Handwriting
PSYCHOLOGY

Handwriting PSYCHOLOGY

PERSONALITY REFLECTED IN HANDWRITING

DR. HELMUT PLOOG

HANDWRITING PSYCHOLOGY
PERSONALITY REFLECTED IN HANDWRITING

iUniverse books may be ordered through booksellers or by contacting:

iUniverse
1663 Liberty Drive
Bloomington, IN 47403
www.iuniverse.com
1-800-Authors (1-800-288-4677)

Because of the dynamic nature of the Internet, any web addresses or links contained in this book may have changed since publication and may no longer be valid. The views expressed in this work are solely those of the author and do not necessarily reflect the views of the publisher, and the publisher hereby disclaims any responsibility for them.

www.graphologie.de

Any people depicted in stock imagery provided by Thinkstock are models, and such images are being used for illustrative purposes only.

Certain stock imagery © Thinkstock.

ISBN: 978-1-4759-7023-4 (sc)
ISBN: 978-1-4759-7022-7 (hc)
ISBN: 978-1-4759-7021-0 (e)

Library of Congress Control Number: 2013900493

Print information available on the last page.

iUniverse rev. date: 05/17/2019

The joy of being a graphologist: discovering the blueprint of a person
with the senses, heart, and mind.
But above all, tracking down the
variety of such blueprints and recognizing
the freedom they give people.

—Helmut Ploog

To my wife Ziling

About the Author

Dr. Helmut Ploog is first chairman of Germany's Professional Association of Certified Graphologists/Psychologists and publishes the journal *Angewandte Graphologie und Persönlichkeitsdiagnostik,* which has been in existence since 1952. This periodical explores applied graphology and character analysis. He regularly organizes the graphology symposium German Graphologists' Day and lectured for many years in handwriting psychology at the University of Munich.

Translator
Sarah Trickey-Volker

Note for Readers
Although all information in this book has been carefully checked, no guarantee of its correctness can be provided.

Table of Contents

Foreword

Graphology or handwriting analysis draws conclusions about the personality of a writer from his or her handwriting. Here, script is considered as body language at the level of fine-motor skills. As body language can be interpreted, graphology forms part of the psychology of expression or diagnostic psychology.

Graphology as a science has developed in Europe for a century or so and is widespread, particularly in Germany, France, Italy, Belgium, Holland, and Switzerland. Its teachings, like all fundamental findings, remain up-to-date and applicable today.

Even the layman is able to distinguish between unformed children's writings, adult handwriting, the scripts of aged or sick people, and the scripts of those suffering from addictions. Alterations in the mental state brought about by hypnosis, the use of medication, or the result of psychotherapy also find expression in handwriting.

Whereas most graphology manuals date from the 1950s and 1960s, this book was rewritten in 1997–98 and underwent complete revision for the English-language version in 2012, including the addition of new handwritings, almost all originating from the English-speaking world. It offers an introduction to the fascinating world of handwriting and allows the reader to immediately implement his newly acquired knowledge. The reader, however, will discover that describing a person in a "graphological report" is extremely difficult and takes years of practice. A word of warning here: the aim is not to pass judgment on another person without due consideration but to take the stance of an observer who analyzes the seismographic swings of a handwriting and finds confirmation in reality.

The author wishes you every success and enjoyment in working through this book, possibly also prompting you to study the subject further. However, do not forget: graphology as a method does not require you merely to acquire knowledge but in addition to learn a skill that calls not only for talent but also for a certain amount of practice.

Dr. Helmut Ploog
former lecturer in handwriting psychology, University of Munich

1

Grasping the totality of a writing is the
most important aspect of graphology.

—J. J. Wittenberg

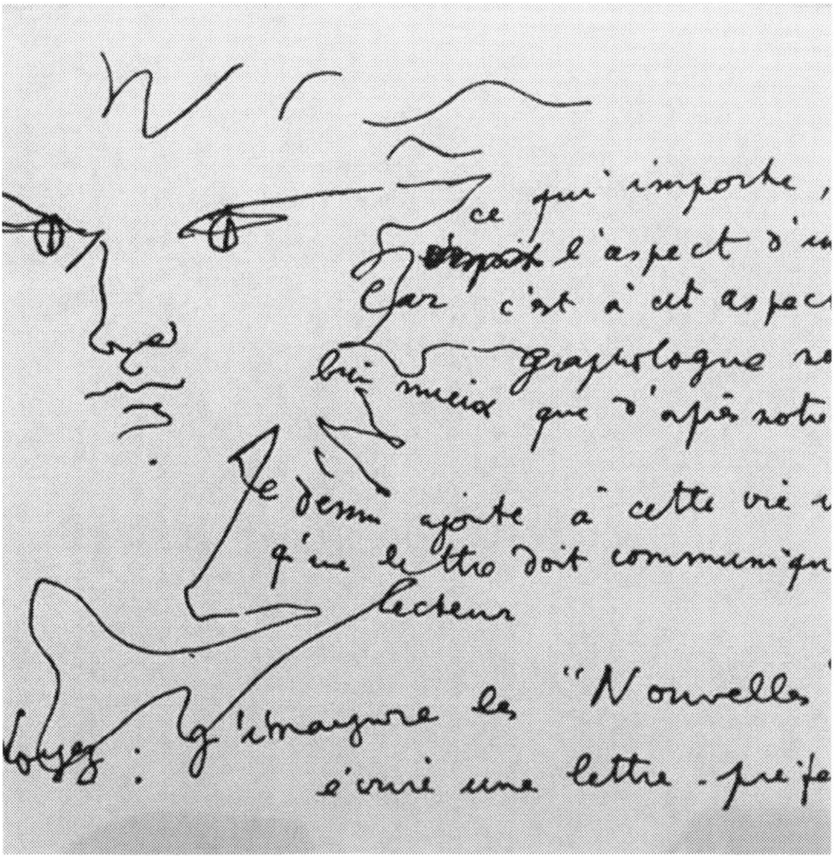

ce qui importe ,
l'aspect
Car c'est à cet
graphologue
bien mieux que d'après
lecteur
"Nouvelles
écrire une lettre

Introduction

POSSIBILITIES AND LIMITS OF GRAPHOLOGY

Handwriting analysis normally allows us to draw reliable conclusions about

- general personality (aims in life/guiding principles, level, quality, structure, transparency, and prospects for development or unrealized potential);

- intelligence;

- strength of will (vitality, temperament, energy, motivation, and ability to achieve);

- social skills (extroversion/introversion, team spirit, attitude toward colleagues, emotional response); and

- reliability (correctness, honesty, and trustworthiness).

Handwriting does not reveal the following:

- **physical features** (bodily strength, height/weight, color of hair/ eyes, or illnesses)

- **facts** (age, sex, past experiences, financial status, or destiny)

- **intellectual particulars** (profession; special skills and knowledge, for example, in the arts, science, or politics; or whether one is a genius)

If the writer does not write very often, has no talent for penmanship, or even suffers from inhibitions in this regard, these factors will make analysis far more difficult in terms of handwriting psychology. This also applies to strictly disciplined scripts or aesthetically stylized handwritings, which do not provide for individual expression by the writer.

Difference in Test Methods

"The origin of testing stems from the needs of higher instances and can be pinpointed as first occurring at a specific moment in time. Graphology on the other hand has come about over the centuries through fluid sources of observation and reflection prompted by handwriting: in a certain sense graphology invented itself. This has allowed it to develop freely without being tied to any specific purpose or confined by specific themes." These are the words of the graphologist Hans Knobloch.[1]

Graphology is not a test in the sense of being a standardized procedure but rather is a technique of evaluating and interpreting the character of the writer. (This does not, however, mean that graphology as a method has failed to measure up to the criteria of reliability and validity prevailing in the field of psychology.[2])

---

1 Hans Knobloch, *Was verrät uns die Handschrift* (Munich/Zurich: Piper, 1991), 10.

2 Readers with an interest in this field are referred to the following dissertation at the University of Bonn, which offers a comprehensive overview: Rainer Doubrawa, "Handschrift und Persönlichkeit," (Frankfurt: Verlag Peter Lang, 1978). [ISBN 3-261-02503-4]

If we compare the practicality of various diagnostic methods, many aptitude studies, psychometric tests, and so on prove to be inferior to graphological analysis because of their intricacy and their cost in terms of both time and money.

Handwriting psychology and test psychology overlap or complement each other in their subject matter and methods involved. They stem from different traditions: test psychology originates more from the natural sciences, and handwriting psychology from the humanities.

A graphological analysis is an interpretation of complete elements in a writer's life, whereas testing involves individual, partial measurements. A test can frequently be evaluated using relatively mechanical methods, whereas graphological interpretation calls for a high level of talent and training in analyzing expression as well as a knowledge of personality theories. But anyone performing a psychology test also needs to be able to assess the effects of a writer's skills and character on specific professional situations.

The diagnostic viewpoint taken by graphology is wider than even that taken with a whole series of tests, thereby justifying the special position of graphology in relation to other psychodiagnostic tests. The graphological picture of personality is an ideal framework for incorporating other findings established through tests, interviews, and so on.

If handwriting samples from different periods of a writer's life are examined, graphology can provide an overview of the individual's entire life. Although there are studies in American psychology in which certain characteristics (the "Big Five") are traced over decades, no consideration is given to the maturity of the subject or successful self-realization. As in all cases where personal development is not completed, the tragedy here is an "unfulfilled life," that is, the failure to take advantage of the opportunities available.

Recruitment tests administered to job applicants take place in a laboratory-type setting. It is known that if people frequently undergo such tests, they can learn to give the "correct" responses, thereby falsifying the test results. Written documents, on the other hand, are the result of a single process in which the writer concentrates on *communication* and not on *writing*. With their handwriting, people unconsciously leave behind a picture of themselves.

Like psychoanalysis, graphology has great difficulty in finding recognition as a science. This is because people do not consider that subjective empathy and interpretation can be reconciled with a specific requirement of natural science, namely that any influence by the observer on the process must be ruled out.

Numerous American tests involving detailed questionnaires bring back to Europe the ideas already developed by C. G. Jung before the Second World War regarding personality types, functions, and attitudes. The basic mind-set of a person is shown very clearly in his or her handwriting.

Graphology considers personality as a functional—or in case of a personality disorder as a dysfunctional—unit. No other diagnostic tool in psychology offers a perspective comparable to graphology.

This excludes any direct and isolated graphological judgment on single "traits".

Difference between Graphology and Questioned Document Examination

Whereas graphology involves evaluating handwriting characteristics with the aim of assessing a writer's personality, questioned document examination is carried out on all kinds of handwritten texts to determine the actual factual particulars involved in each case. In other words, it is performed to verify signatures on contracts of sale, checks, and receipts; to establish the authenticity of wills and testaments; or to check the identity of the author of anonymous letters against a possible suspect. Here the process does not generally involve just making a comparison between writings but examining the entire document in relation to the paper and ink used, as well as alterations, additions, erasures, and so on. The procedure for such examination is laid down in ASTM Standard E444-98 (Standard Description of Scope of Work Relating to Forensic Document Examination).

In general the handwriting expert is confronted with relatively obvious efforts at dissimulation, as very few writers are able to fully disguise their scripts.

The graphologist Patricia Siegel stated:

> Traditionally and typically, handwriting experts prepare exhibits for court in which individual letters and words from questioned and known writing samples are cut out and placed side by side on a single board. The experts want the judge or jury's attention to be focused on specifically narrow areas of comparison. Exhibits clarify testimony and allow the court to better understand the basis for an expert's opinion.[3]

But as the past has shown, no handwriting expert is infallible!

Lengthy training is required to qualify as a questioned document examiner, as is extensive practical experience. Although many graphologists also work as questioned document examiners in countries such as Italy and Spain, a much stricter distinction is made between the two professions in the USA, the United Kingdom, and Germany. In these countries specialists have not generally trained in graphology beforehand and therefore have to first slowly find their way about the world of handwriting and its jargon.

Admission to the profession is normally controlled by individual professional organizations:

---

3   Patricia Siegel, "Value of Graphological Training for the Handwriting Identification Expert," *Journal of the American Society of Professional Graphologists* 4, (Winter 1995/96): 104.

- American Society of Questioned Document Examiners (ASQDE)—USA

- Forensic Science Society (FSS)—United Kingdom

- Gesellschaft für Forensische Schriftuntersuchung (GFS)—Germany

The following are some well-known cases from the history of questioned document examination:

- the Dreyfus affair (1894)

- the Lindbergh kidnapping (1934)

- the Clifford Irving forgery (1972)

- the Howard Hughes Mormon will (1978)

- the Hitler Diaries (1983)

History of Graphology

Graphology was first mentioned by the Roman historian Sueton some two thousand years ago. Here he was speaking about the handwriting of Augustus, commenting that the words were incredibly close together, without the amount of space normally left between words. In the Far East as well, people have always believed that a person's character is revealed by his or her writing, and it is significant that they speak of an ink trail as "coming from the heart."

Systematic graphology, however, did not become possible until individual handwritings came into being. It was only with the gradual disappearance of the ornamental handwritings in the Renaissance period that the first book about graphology was published, a treatise written by a professor of medicine from Bologna, Camillo Baldi. Other works followed from adherents of handwriting and amateur graphologists, from Goethe through Lavater to Alexander von Humboldt.

In the second half of the nineteenth century the term *graphology* was coined in France by Abbé **Jean-Hippolyte Michon** (1806–1881). It comes from the Greek, consisting of the words *graphein* ("to write") and *logos* ("word, study,"). His most important work, *System of Graphology*,[4] was not translated into German until 1965.

Michon took an empirical approach to his work. He tried to group together handwriting characteristics of people known to him so that such categorizations could be linked to specific personality traits. Many of the interpretations established by Michon are still valid today. His graphological system, incidentally, reflected the picture of man held in that day and age—that is, the human psyche was seen as the sum of clear-cut characteristics.

In France, Michon's system was developed further by **Jules Crépieux-Jamin** (1858–1940), in particular by the introduction of the degree of harmony present in handwriting as a general feature.[5] He was the godfather of French graphology, and his system forms the basis of the French method even today.

In Germany, it was mainly psychiatrists and physiologists who were interested in graphology during this period. **Wilhelm Preyer** (1841–1897) interpreted handwriting as the result of impulses from the cortex of the brain. **Georg Meyer** (1869–1917) investigated the handwriting of patients with bipolar disorder and confirmed his working hypothesis that the characteristics of one's handwriting have a psychological basis. The year 1896 saw the founding of the Deutsche Graphologische Gesellschaft in Munich, which soon numbered 300 members based all over the world. They adopted a wide range of approaches to their research into the expressive value of handwriting for application in terms of graphology.

Ludwig Klages (1872–1956) was to German graphology what Crépieux-Jamin was to French—he is considered the founder of scientific graphology

---

4   J. H. Michon, *System der Graphologie* (Munich: Ernst Reinhardt, 1965).

5   J. Crépieux-Jamin, *Die Grundlagen der Graphologie* (Heidelberg: Niels Kampmann,1927).

in Germany. He left behind an impressive number of publications and adherents, who still uphold his beliefs today via the association Klages-Gesellschaft e.V., based at Marbach am Neckar.

Klages defined handwriting as the lasting manifestation of the personal writing movement. His most important work, *Handschrift und Charakter,* was already published in 1916, with the twenty-ninth edition last appearing in 1989. According to Klages, the specific meaning of individual writing elements is not lexically fixed but has to be determined instead through dynamic psychological analysis of the writing process and structure in terms of expression and personality.

All elements of writing and their corresponding character traits have a double meaning. Whether this is positive or negative in each case depends on the individual configuration of elements and, in particular, the quality of the handwriting as a whole—in other words the so-called form level or rhythm of the script. This principle of graphology is still used today.

A different approach was applied by **Max Pulver** (1889–1952) from Switzerland, a system that was clearly demonstrated by the title of his most important publication: *Symbolism of Handwriting.* He lectured in graphology at the University of Zurich and was able to apply the findings of depth psychology to the interpretation of handwriting. For him the different directions involved in writing movement—that is, toward the top/bottom and left/right of the page—formed a system of spatial coordinates that symbolized the essence of a writer.

Another book, *The Soul and Handwriting,* the most significant work of the graphologist **Ania Teillard**, was based on the analytical psychology of C. G. Jung. Even today it ranks as one of the ten most important works of graphology.

Rudolf Pophal (1893–1966), who originally trained in the field of medicine, carried out a detailed investigation into the basic motor-physiological aspects of writing movement. He developed a system defining the degrees of tension apparent in writing, which could then be interpreted accordingly. Although neurology has since departed from these principles, the categories established by Pophal are still used successfully in German graphology today.

Robert Heiss (1903–1974) was the director of the Institute for Psychology at the University of Freiburg. In his method of graphology he distinguished between three aspects in writing: movement, form, and space, a system that has also been adopted in this book. In other words, the writing element is produced through a writing process that comes into being as a movement in space and manifests itself as a form as it progresses. Incidentally, it was Heiss who postulated, at the first postwar conference of the Association of German Psychologists held in 1947, that a writer should no longer be seen as a conglomerate of characteristics or a structure but as a process that is never complete. If we consider the writing of an individual at different stages of his life according to this basic attitude, our assessment will automatically acquire greater depth and dynamism.

Many graphological researchers had to leave Europe during the era of Nazism—**Rudolph S. Hearns, Hans Jacoby, Alfred Kanfer, Felix Klein, Alfred Mendel, Richard Pokorny, Klara G. Roman, Ulrich Sonnemann, Thea Stein Lewinson, Herry O. Teltscher, Frank Victor, and Werner Wolff**—landing in either the USA or Palestine. They were unfortunately not able to broaden the influence of graphology through their activities in the United States and ensure it was recognized at an academic level. Only Thea Stein Lewinson, who worked for the CIA for many years, had any success here, setting up the American Society of Professional Graphologists (www.aspghandwriting.org), which is still active today in New York.

Another important graphologist was **Roda Wieser** (1894–1986), who, like Klages, saw rhythm as a benchmark for personality. She interpreted the fundamental rhythm of handwriting as a cosmic aspect. "This cosmic reality thus also includes the integrated ego of man, which we experience in the quality of the strong fundamental rhythm apparent in a writing."[6]

---

6   R. Wieser, *Handschrift, Rhythmus, Persönlichkeit: eine graphologische Bilanz* (Bonn: Bouvier, 1989), 142. Please also see issue 175 of the French journal *La Graphologie* dated July 1984, which shows the handwriting of almost all the important graphologists from the last 100 years.

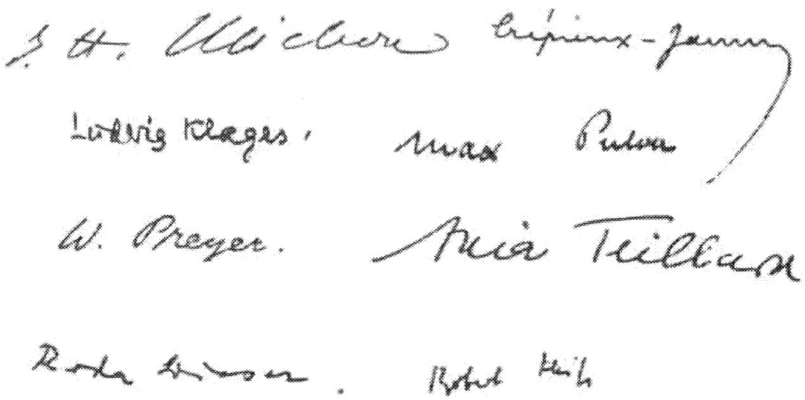

Fig. 1 Handwriting of well-known graphologists

School Copybook and Individuality in Handwriting

In the world of graphology, handwriting is above all meaningful from the viewpoint of handwriting psychology when the writer shows a certain degree of individuality—that is, departs from the school copybook model. Children are first taught print script, followed by cursive writing. However, in the USA, penmanship has not been included in the curriculum of studies for new teachers for several decades. Students often merely write emulative cursive instead of real cursive. Once children have attained a certain level of fluency at around age nine, it is essential that they adapt the forms and proportions of handwriting in line with their own personality. In so doing, they demonstrate personal development and maturity. It is only then that their writing will acquire not only a communicative character but also an expressive character. But if graphologists are to correctly identify such changes, they must be familiar with the school model script or "copybook" taught at the child's elementary school.

The universal applicability of graphology can also be seen in the fact that writers show similar deviations from the copybook model regardless of their nationality and system of characters: circles used as i-dots, left slant, and imprecise letters and lines are not found in any copybook model, yet can be observed in writers from widely differing backgrounds.

There are an infinite number of examples here: unraveling, thready letter forms, exaggerated lower lengths, falling or rising lines, and so on. Writers deviate from the school copybook without being aware of this, prompting Werner Wolff to describe handwriting as a "diagram of the unconscious."

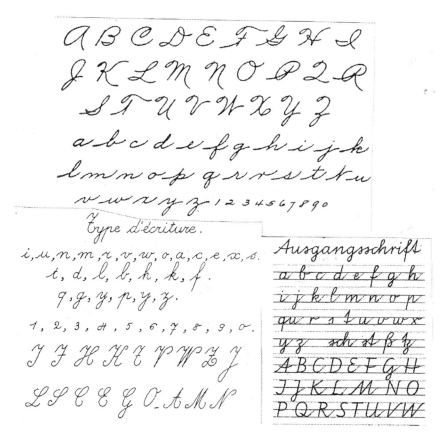

Fig. 2 Copybook models of USA, France and Germany

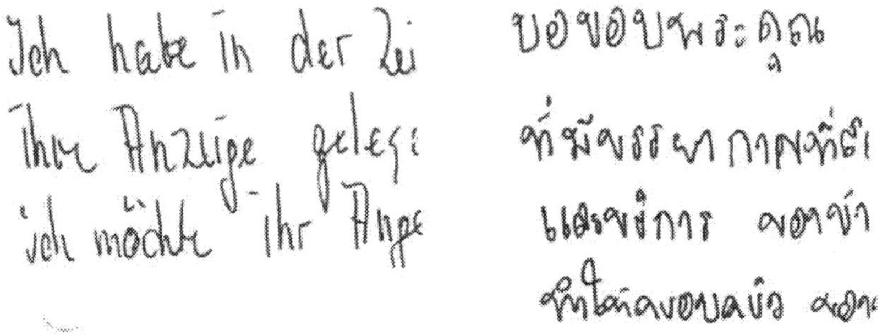

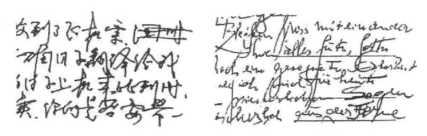

Fig. 3 Leftward slant in the handwriting of a German and Thai writer

Fig. 4 Disturbed layout in the handwriting of a
Chinese person and a Portuguese person.

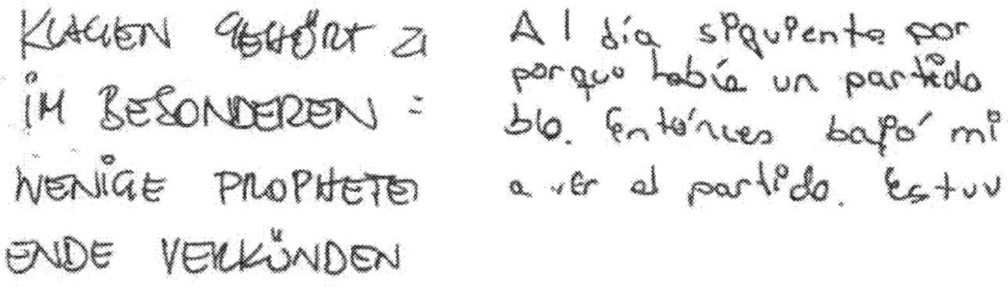

Fig. 5 I-dots as circles in the handwriting of an adult (the director of a circus)
and a thirteen-year-old Spanish girl

2

*May he repeatedly practice on new samples of
handwriting and he will at last reach his goal: he can
interpret its movement with his eye as the trained
musician hears the sound of a melody just by looking at the score.*

—B. Christiansen and E. Carnap

General Impression of Writing

First Impression

Handwriting analysis starts with acquiring a first impression of the writing. The script is contemplated without any preconceptions, where possible ignoring any positive or negative perceptions. Here it is best if graphologists allow a writing to work on them, letting their attention "float" over it without any particular focus. It sometimes helps to retrace the actual strokes of the writer's pen in order to actively experience the movements originally made.

The first impression made by the writing may relate to the appearance of the script overall, which may look spontaneous, genuine, artificial, or stylized. However, it is recommended that one break down the characteristic elements of the general impression so as to establish areas that are dominant or neglected.

The first impression allows us to distinguish between four characteristic picture types. The following list is intended to act only as an aid in this regard, as there are no limits on what the graphologist may notice in the writing.

Overall picture types

Movement picture: Lively, deft, hesitant, flowing, expansive, skillful, faltering, streaming, running, brash, brisk, strong, weak, bubbly, held back, agile, smooth, sure, creeping, sweeping, sluggish, dragging, raging, carefree.

Stroke picture: Colorful, colorless, juicy, dry, relaxed, firm, dense, spongy, pure, uneven, granulated, amorphous, vibrant, dead, elastic, limp, smeary, tremulous.

Form picture: Bizarre, simple, delicate, large, round, lavish, thin, puffed up, squat, artificial, natural, original, affected, evolved, structured, carefully formed, personalized, individual, skilled, refined, independent.

Space picture: Wide, narrow, woven, structured, even, ragged, ordered, matted, dense, sparse, weblike, with gaps, clear, clearly spaced.

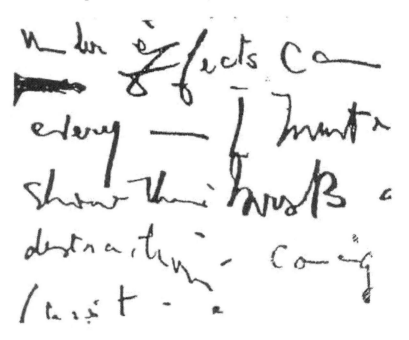

Fig. 6 This handwriting gives the impression of being disharmonious, torn, and choppy.

The handwriting above helps to illustrate how the descriptive terms listed are applied.

It is clear here that the overall impression is determined by the *prevalence of movement*. The impressionistic description of the four pictures results in the following characterization:

- **Movement picture:** disturbed, abrupt, agitated, restless, impulsive, nervous, powerful

- **Stroke picture:** distinct, colorful, granulated, plastic, intense, dense

- **Form picture:** disturbed, neglected, bizarre, fantastic, contradictory

- **Space picture:** disturbed, carefree, wide, sweeping, torn, muddled, chaotic

The idea of looking at a handwriting sample through the three prisms of movement, form, and space has become a central concept in German graphology:

> "Heiss differentiated three global processes intermingling while writing: the motoric, bringing about the Picture of Movement, the organizational—creating the Picture of Space, and the design of letter shapes, depicted in the Picture of Form. Each of these handwriting perspectives, viewed as Gestalts, shows a different developmental pattern throughout the lifespan and relates to different, well-defined, personality aspects. Movement reflects temperament, the inner drives, emotions and moods. Space relates to the adjustment to one's environment and the creation of a personal space within it, based also on organizational skills. The formal elements show awareness of one's culture and ideals, cognitive processing of information and the overt style of behavior."[7]

In graphology we also use *typologies,* which can be considered indicators of personality—for example, the types, functions, and attitudes

---

7   Dafna Yalon, "The Larger Picture," *Global Graphology* (May 2004): 33.

according to C. G. Jung, the temperaments according to Hippocrates, Maslow's hierarchy of needs, or classification into life forms as used by Spranger. In this introduction to graphology we can deal only with this last typology, which looks at values in terms of objectives. Regarding the ideal type,[8] Spranger recognized six life forms that can be seen in writing:

Life Form	Cultural Area	Value
Theoretical	Science	Findings, truth
Aesthetic	Art	Desire for form, expression
Power	Politics	Power and control
Social	Society	Love and help
Economical	Economics/business	Benefit
Religious	Religion	Fulfillment of purpose of life

Table of Characteristic Elements

Theoretical Type	Aesthetic Type	Power Type	Social Type	Economical Type	Religious Type
Clear, precise, objective, intellectual, succinct	Soft, carefully formed, stylized, gentle, refined	Hard, forceful, tense, angular, sure	Open, free, natural, simple, possibly copybook	Quick, simplified, expansive, free, uninhibited, independent	Not clearly identifiable from handwriting
Figs. 23, 24	Figs. 54, 95	Figs. 41, 65	Figs. 60, 63	Fig. 11	-

Fig. 7 Life forms according to Spranger.

Individual features of relevance are of course also taken into account here for classification of each type.

---

8 E. Spranger, *Lebenforman* (Tübingen: Max Niemeyer, 1966). [

Form or Movement

When considering the general impression made by a handwriting, we have already looked at the picture of form and movement. Here it is possible that writing is dominated by either form or movement. This is illustrated in the figures shown below:

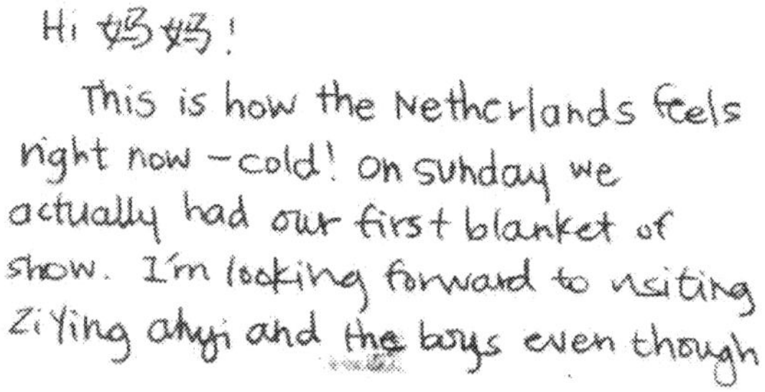

Hi 🌸🌸!

This is how the Netherlands feels
right now – cold! On Sunday we
actually had our first blanket of
snow. I'm looking forward to visiting
Ziying ahyi and the boys even though

Fig. 8 Prevalence of form is shown in the handwriting of a female law student.

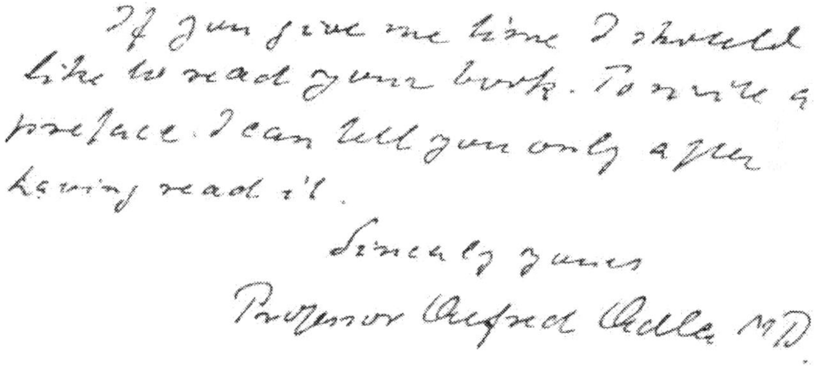

[handwriting sample of Alfred Adler]

Fig. 9 Prevalence of movement is shown in the modest and sensitive handwriting of psychologist Alfred Adler.

In practice, the distinction from one extreme to the other is often not clear-cut. However, what counts here are the overlapping aspects that occur independently of the individual elements in a writing, yet have an effect. This is why the graphologists Müller and Enskat[9] also speak of "overlapping findings."

---

9   W. H. Müller and A. Enskat, *Graphologische Diagnostik,* 2nd ed. (Bern/Stuttgart/

> An emphasis on movement in one's handwriting reveals the extent to which the writer is ruled by unconscious feelings and impulses, affected by spontaneous direct reactions.
>
> An emphasis on form in a writing shows the level of a writer's consciousness , revealing the guiding forces and demands of the superego, whether they are appropriate for the writer or not.

The ideal is a writing that looks rhythmic, in which the form is carried easily by the movement without becoming distorted in any way.

Form Level

Above we mentioned the expression *form level* (FL), a term that was used in the lexicon of graphology by Ludwig Klages.[10] Once again this concept does not relate to individual elements but the overall aspect of the script. It represents the degree of individuality and originality of a sample of writing. Although the expression *form level* is rejected by some experts, it is still of great use today. Experienced graphologists generally have no problem in reaching agreement about the form level of a person's writing.

Form level is determined by the following elements:

rhythm (rhythm of movement, form, and space) + originality

By rhythm of space (or distribution) we mean the impression of balance made on the written page. The rhythm of movement describes whether the flow of movement is disrupted—that is, expansive movements in ragged handwriting will reduce its form level. The rhythm of form relates to the balance seen in spontaneously produced letterforms.

Vienna:Huber, 1973).

10   L. Klages, *Handschrift und Character,* 24th ed., (Bonn: Bouvier, 1956).

Any exaggeration—such as decoration or enrichment—will reduce the form level. We can therefore say the following: the greater the individuality shown by a person's handwriting, the more personalized the individual letterforms will be. The more natural, original, and evolved they look, the more positive and the higher the degree of organization—that is, the form level—will be. To use an expression from the French mime artist Marcel Marceau, the "weight of the soul" *(le poids de l'âme)* reveals itself in the form level.

A high form level can be identified by the strong rhythm and individuality of the writing, and a low form level by weak rhythm and lack of individuality.

Handwritings with a high form level look dynamic, unconventional, and original, whereas writings with a low form level look dull, stereotyped, and banal.

Form level can be divided into five degrees—that is, evaluated according to the German system for grading schoolwork, ranging from 1 (high form level) to 5 (low form level).

Form level 1

Level 1, Dr. Gille and I are unfortunately in agreement with your quoting M. Delamain's ; level is 2-3 at most. Furthermore the produced evinces a few discrete marks of isorganization.

Form level 1–2

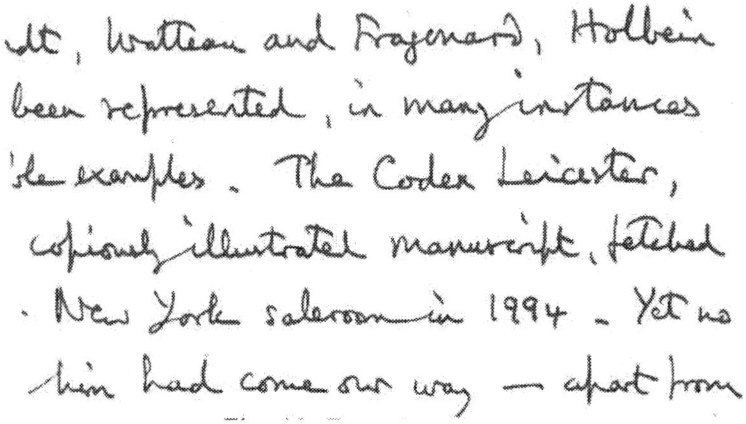

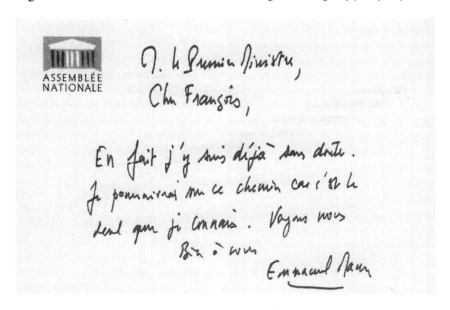

Fig. 10 Form level 1: The second handwriting has a slightly jerky rhythm.

Fig. 11 Form level 2 shows original and condensed forms in the handwriting of the French president E. Macron.

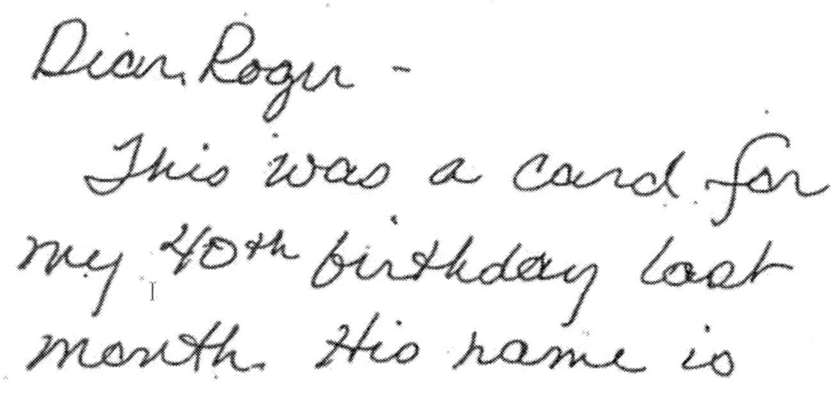

Fig. 12 Form level 3: disturbed rhythm of movement and copybook forms

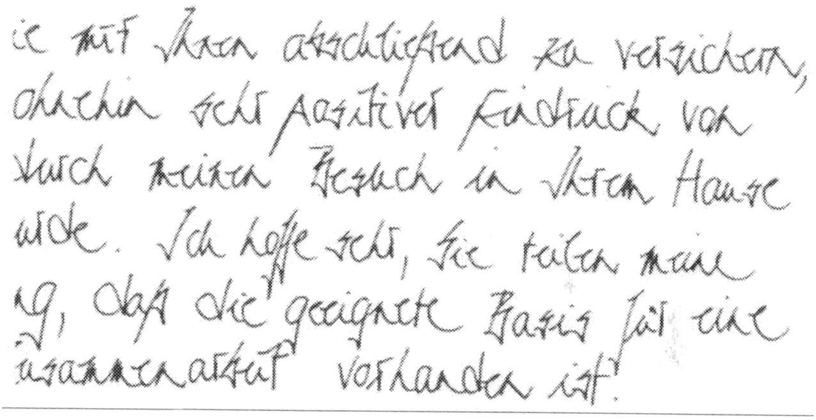

Fig. 13 Form level 4: strangely stylized writing
of a thirty-four-year-old woman

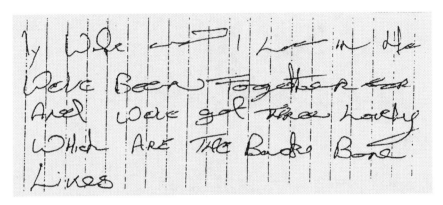

Fig. 14 Anarchic writing and movement over form.

Other examples for the evaluation of form level in the writings included in this manual are as follows: FL 1 = Figs. 9, 33, 95; FL 2 = Figs. 24, 41, 43; FL 3 = Figs. 19, 22, 52; FL 4 = Figs. 39, 81, 82, 83, 89.

Numerous books have already been written about the periodic rhythm of handwriting (in contrast to the beat of a metronome). The author Roda Wieser even sees a cosmic aspect to this, understanding and perceiving man in his quality as a cosmic being. "Through the apparent quality of the polar rhythm we see, experience and interpret other human beings in line with man and the cosmos according to reality."[11]

Graphologists believe it is possible to identify the extent to which the cosmic power of human consciousness is realized from the intellectuality and spirituality of rhythm shown in a person's handwriting (Fig. 9).

---

11   R. Wieser, *Handschrift, Rhythmus, Persönlichkeit* (Bonn: Bouvier, 1989), 142.

3

Handwriting certainly does not reveal everything, but the most
fundamental part of a person, the essence
of his personality so to speak is
shown to us in a snapshot. If we know how
to see and read it, a collection of
handwritings will automatically become for
us a physiognomic knowledge
of the world, a typology of the creative spirit.

—Stefan Zweig

Individual Elements

In our writing system we move from left to right: we could also say from the Me to the You. The lowercase letters form the *middle zone* of a writing. Movements that extend above this level are known as the *upper lengths,* moving away from the writer's body. Similarly, movements that are below the middle zone (g-loops) are known as the *lower lengths,* moving from the baseline toward the writer's body. Strokes that extend above and below the middle zone are called upper and lower lengths.

The *middle zone* of a handwriting represents the writer's ego, whereas the *upper zone* stands for the mind and intellect and the *lower zone* for the individual's instincts and drives and the material world.

The threefold division into body, mind, and soul can thus be translated to handwriting.

1. Space Picture

Size of Handwriting

The size of a person's handwriting is an obvious feature that is often altered when documents are forged by fraudsters. Size may also depend on other factors such as poor eyesight, age, or disease—for example, the microscopic handwritings seen in patients suffering from Parkinson's.

However, in principle, graphologists assume that the size of a person's handwriting remains more or less constant, like its other features. If the middle zone of a writing (for example, the letters *a, m, n, r, w,* and so on) exceeds 3 mm by more than 10 percent, we say it is large handwriting. If they are less than 2.5 mm in size, the handwriting is described as small. The upper and lower lengths are not taken into consideration here.

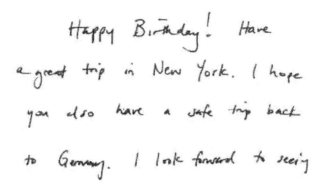

Fig. 15 Small handwriting

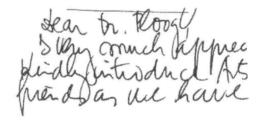

Fig. 16 Large handwriting that also shows a strong emphasis on movement with tangling lines

The size of a person's handwriting may be basically interpreted in relation to two aspects: the development of will and personality vis-à-vis the environment and the writer's self-esteem. Large handwriting is seen as expansion, an unfolding into space. Experience has shown that in female writers self-esteem can be seen in a large middle zone, whereas in men the middle zone tends to be small.

To help with understanding, plus and minus signs have been used in the following tables to indicate that positive or negative characteristics are involved in each case. However, it is ultimately up to the reader to reach a conclusion in this regard.

Table 1 Size of middle zone as an expression of will

	Large	Small
+	Enthusiasm, drive toward expansion, willingness to act, activity, urge for self-assertion and influence	Objective concentration, sense of reality, sober moderation, little urge toward expansion
-	Unceasing activity, weak grasp of reality, naivete, impulsivity	Lack of dynamism, passivity, inhibition

Negative interpretations arise from the overall context of the handwriting, for example, especially in relation to the form level or conspicuous and extreme movements such as exaggerated size and expansive movements or in the case of small handwriting, rigidity of movement and excessive stiffness.

Table 2 Size of middle zone as an expression of self-esteem

	Large	Small
+	Self-confidence/certainty, emotional demands, need for attention, pathos	Modesty, not demanding, no wish to be the center of attention
-	Superiority, arrogance, self-presentation	Insecurity, feeling of inferiority, depression

Special elements:

1. Ends of words decreasing in size: waning effort, impatience, diplomatic adaptation

2. Ends of words increasing in size: greater self-assertion, naively forced effort and urge for influence

3. Irregular size in middle zone: fluctuating feelings of self-esteem

4. Extremely small handwriting: fear of reality

Fig. 17 Ends of words decreasing and increasing in size

Width of Writing

In graphology the width of a person's handwriting is understood to refer to the distance between the individual letters. Width more or less the same size as the height of the letters is considered normal letter spacing.

Width in writing is generally produced by a movement to the right and points toward expansion of drives and relaxation. Narrowness, on the other hand, is caused by restrictions on free movement, inhibition of drives, and increased tension.

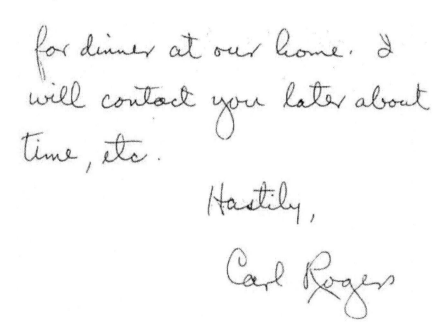

Fig. 18 The handwriting of psychologist Carl Rogers is small and wide.

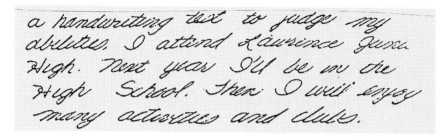

Fig. 19 Narrow handwriting

If the type of connection is also taken into consideration, width in combination with curves points toward an ability to empathize, whereas width and angles with a right slant are an indication of determination. Handwriting that also has heavy pressure shows a tendency toward self-assertion. It is therefore necessary to consider a whole number of elements in conjunction with each other before making an interpretation.

Whereas the width of the individual letters is a sign of self-confidence, the spacing between letters represents the writer's relationship with his environment. Here width can be analyzed from the aspects of both space and movement.

Table 3 Width as expansion toward the outer world or a desire for space

	Wide	**Narrow**
+	Ambition, determination, openness, interest in outside world, lack of inhibition, forward-looking	Self-control/restraint, caution, concentration
-	Impatience, unwillingness to commit, evasion, excessive demands	Lack of inner freedom, inhibition, anxiety, lack of directness

Special elements:

1. Alternation between width and narrowness: unbalanced relationship to outer world; when seen with variations in size and slant, also inner uncertainty

2. Ends of words becoming wider: lack of stamina and consistency

3. Ends of words becoming narrower: caution and restraint acquired through experience

4. Narrow letters and wide letter spacing (secondary width): correctness and striving for order, forced concentration, self-control, possible tendency toward formalistic thinking

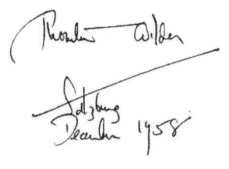

Fig. 20 Example of secondary width

Proportions

In graphology a distinction is made between the *division in length* of a person's handwriting—that is, the ratio between the upper and the lower length, and the *difference in length*—that is, the ratio between the upper/lower lengths and the middle zone.

Division in length

Both the upper and the lower lengths can be either exaggerated or stunted. Likewise, a writer may fail to observe the ratio given by the copybook between the long letters (with upper and lower length) and the short letters (without upper and lower length). The copybook defines a ratio of 1:2:3 as short length = 1, upper length = 2, long length = 3.

This is illustrated by the following figures:

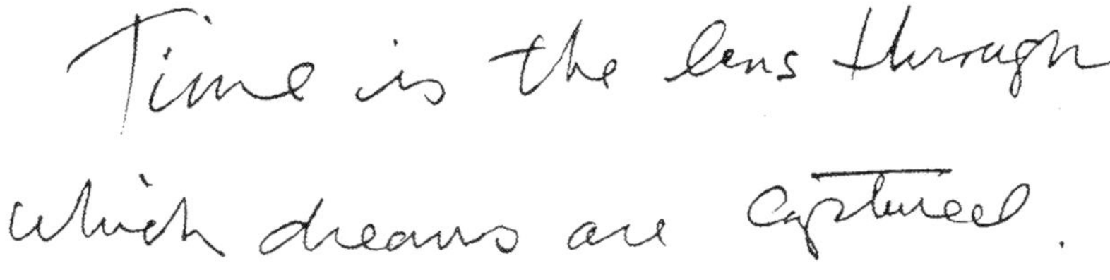

Time is the lens through which dreams are captured.

Fig. 21 Emphasis on upper lengths in the handwriting of a film director

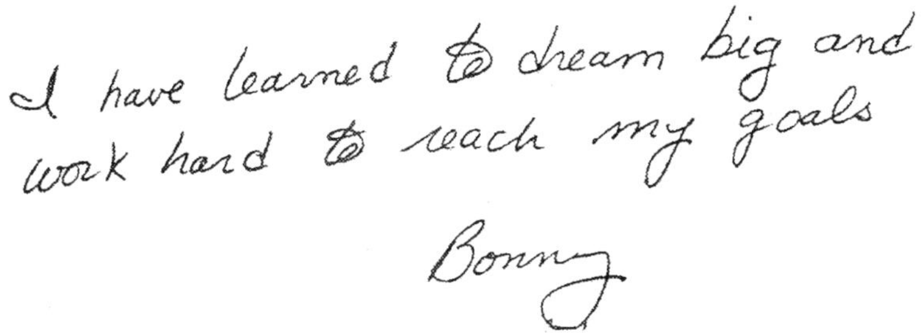

I have learned to dream big and work hard to reach my goals

Bonny

Fig. 22 Emphasis on lower lengths in the handwriting of a female pilot

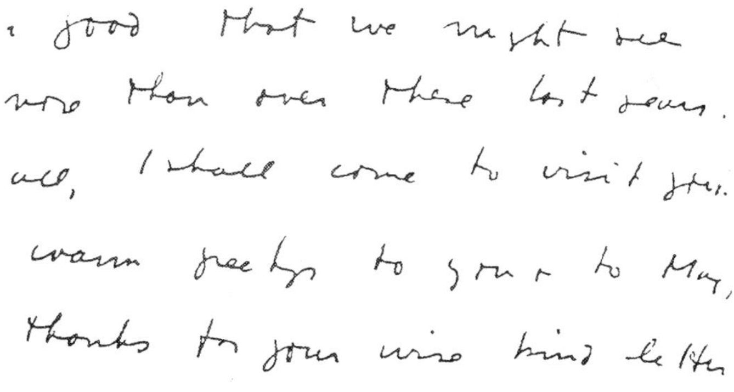

Fig. 23 The simplified handwriting with a neglected lower zone of physicist Robert Oppenheimer

In practice the variations may be more or less pronounced. In other words, the lower or upper lengths are extremely large in some cases, and others are small or stunted.

The interpretation of emphasis on the lower or upper lengths is based on the symbolism of space, with the upper zone representing the intellect, mind, and spirit, and the lower zone the vital, the specific, and the practical. If a person's handwriting shows a good balance in terms of proportions, it can be assumed that there is a stable relationship between the strivings of the ego and the outside world.

Table 4 Ratio between the upper and lower lengths as an expression of the writer's orientation toward the intellectual or the material world

	Emphasis on upper lengths	**Emphasis on lower lengths**
+	Idealistic, spiritual striving, less interest in the mundane and everyday matters	Practical, traditional, firmly rooted, interest in technical/financial matters
-	Exaggeration, fantasy, unrealistic attitudes	Materialism, strongly affected by drives/instincts, stagnation

Special elements:

1. Upper lengths atrophied: lack of intellectual/spiritual tendencies, impetus

2. Lower lengths atrophied: weak instincts/drives, no firm roots or sublimation of drives

3. Triangular lower lengths: willful; wish to dominate; self-assertion, including within small groups

4. Lower lengths broken off: suppression of drives, disassociation from drives, disorders

5. Upper lengths flattened or buckled: dejection as the basic attitude toward life, personal sensitivity

6. Inflated upper lengths (larger than initial letters): delusional, little sense of reality, possibly deceit

Regarding the generally held view that sizable lower lengths are an indication of sexual responsiveness, it should be noted that the pressure and pastiness of the script are also of significance here; otherwise it would be a case of the "spirit being willing but the flesh weak," with these features pointing toward the vitality of a writer.

In this context we should also mention the form of lower lengths known as the lyrical curve. This left-tending garland, which is often found in the writing of poets, reveals a tendency toward the aesthetic.

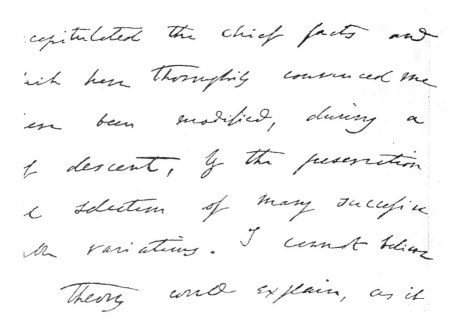

Fig. 24 The handwriting of Charles Darwin shows a lyrical curve in the g.

Difference in length

Differences in length are contrasts in size in handwriting—that is, the ratio between the long letters (with upper and lower length) to the short letters. The normal ratio according to the copybook model should be in the order of 3:2:1. Minor differences in length result in a large middle zone (Fig. 19), whereas in the opposite case, major differences in length result in a small middle zone (Fig. 18).

The size of the short letters represents the ego, and the upper and lower lengths stand for the environment. The more a person's handwriting extends up and down, the stronger his or her orientation toward objective questions and external goals. A sense of responsibility will dominate at the expense of the self.

Table 5 Difference in length as an expression of orientation toward the self or outside world

	Major differences in length (upper and lower lengths larger than middle zone)	**Minor differences in length** (middle zone larger than upper and lower lengths)
+	Ambitious, expansion, enterprising, dynamic, objective attitude	Focus on what is near, inner calm, contentment, strong family feeling, personal orientation
-	Restless, scatterbrained, "spirit willing but flesh weak," shaky sense of self-esteem	Limited interests, static, little impetus, indifference, stagnation

Special elements:

1. Individual exaggerated long lengths (Fig. 21): emphasis on self through desire to achieve, ambitious objectives

2. Long lengths concave (Figs. 11, 21): perseverance, combating of obstacles

3. Long lengths convex: lack of resistance, easily influenced or discouraged

Slant

In graphology we speak of slant or the angle of a person's handwriting, understood as the angle between the upstroke and downstroke and the baseline. Writing is considered to be upright or vertical when the downstroke forms an angle of 90 degrees with the baseline, right-slanted when this angle is less than 90 degrees, and left-slanted when this angle is greater than 90 degrees. The degree and type of slant represents the writer's orientation toward the outside world.

The different slants can also be compared with the position of a rider on a horse: bent forward corresponds to right-slanted, upright is vertical, and leaning back is left-slanted. Acting as a brake, a left slant is never natural—it is always acquired.

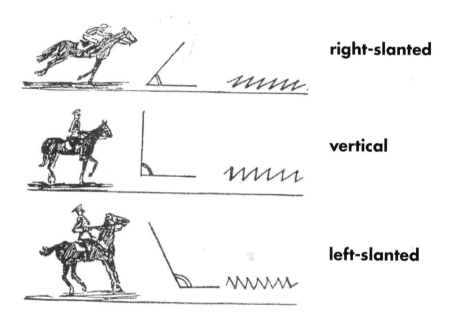

right-slanted

vertical

left-slanted

Fig. 25 As the rider controls the horse, the writer controls his impulses.

We often find a left slant among adolescents, although this normally gives way to right-slanted writing over time.

Special cases such as the frequent left slant of left-handed people or so-called mirror writing are not taken into account here. The slant in the body of a text and the signature may also differ to a greater or lesser degree.

Normally a certain amount of variation is permitted in terms of slant, for example, in the case of vertical handwriting between 85 and

95 degrees. If, on the other hand, 90 percent of all downstrokes are parallel, the slant will appear *rigid*—that is, the handwriting is kept under strict control.

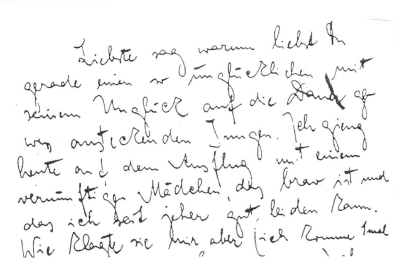

Fig. 26 Left slant and lack of strength in the handwriting of Franz Kafka

More frequently we come across *variable slant,* something that points to a lack of consistency in the writer's relationship with the outside world or a fundamental ambivalence (see Fig. 14). Sometimes there is a change in slant as the writer progresses across the page; it becomes more slanted or vertical at the end of a line or word, an indicator respectively of flagging control or increasing restraint.

Table 6 Slant as an expression of a positive or negative attitude toward the outside world

	Right slant	**Vertical**	**Left slant**
+	Orientation to outside world, commitment to tasks undertaken, engagement, directness	Thoughts kept under control, sober approach, discipline, "stiff upper lip"	Restraint (possibly temporary), willpower, fear of life, strong self-control, protective attitude, in denial about feelings of insecurity
-	Lack of control and restraint, impulsive, rash, easily influenced, frivolous, uncontrolled	Reserve, coldness, passivity, difficult contact with others, inhibited	

A left slant in the handwriting of adults does not necessarily imply a lack of success in their chosen profession.

Special elements:

1. Variable slant: inconsistent, ambivalent, indecisive, changing attitude to outside world

2. Slant becoming more acute at ends of words: spontaneous impulses gain the upper hand, control giving way to feeling of release

3. Slant becoming more vertical at ends of words: becoming less approachable, greater restraint

Layout

The elements of layout in handwriting are as follows:

- Spacing between words

- Spacing between lines

- Direction of lines and

- Margins

The way in which the writer manages the space available on the page depends on conventional and aesthetic considerations, and possibly also an aspect of economy. Basically, a clear layout points to a clarity of mind and sense of organization, as well as to independence and skill in dealing with the outside world.

Word Spacing

This refers to the space left between two words, with normal spacing being more or less the width of one letter. If we see words as units of meaning or concepts, this indicates clear-cut separation and differentiation of thought. However, word spacing can be interpreted at an intellectual as well as at a social level. It also includes man's integration into a community, prompting the graphologist Lutz Wagner to comment, "Just as man fits into the community of people, the word also fits in the community of words."

Large word spacing always indicates a tendency to stand back from emotional events, taking time out for considered thought between impulse and action.

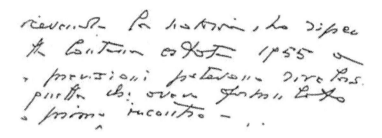

Fig. 27 Wide word spacing is seen in the handwriting of biologist and Nobel Prize winner Rita Levi-Montalcini.

Word and line spacing that is too narrow will result in a less structured writing (see Fig. 22). However, when combined with a good form level or rhythm, it points to a full life and artistic productivity.

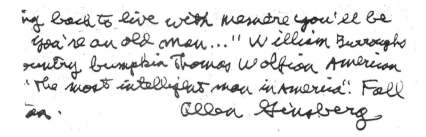

Fig. 28 Narrow line distance and wavy lines characterize the handwriting of Allen Ginsberg.

Table 7 Word spacing: increase in distance and need for a global view

	Large	**Small**
+	Mental clarity, overview, distance between objects and people	Need for contact, directness, thought patterns influenced by previous experiences
-	Emotional inhibition, isolation, difficult contact with others	Lack of distance or mental order, chaotic inner life

Special elements:

1. Wide word spacing with narrow line spacing: outward participation with inner isolation

2. Narrow word spacing with wide line spacing: sociability with a need for space

Line Spacing

As a characteristic of the structure of a person's handwriting, line spacing also forms part of the picture of space. The vertical structuring of the page indicates the writer's attitude toward the world outside.

In terms of time, poor structure relates to an early stage of development—in other words, experience over order. The need for organization corresponds to a later stage of development, that is, order over experience. However, considerations involving aesthetics and guiding images also play a role here.

Line spacing is assessed from the distance between the lower lengths of one line and the upper lengths of the next line. Normal spacing is considered to be the line spacing laid down by the copybook model (1.5 mm). If the upper and lower lengths are caught up with each other, we also speak of tangled lines.

for yr kind message to me wh I have received & read with great pleasure.

Winston S. Churchill

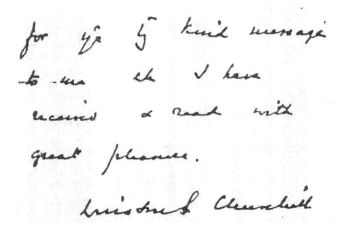

Fig. 29 Straight lines and notable line and word distance in Winston Churchill's handwriting

My parents are enjoying themselves very much but I would like it much better if you were here. I suppose you are just about thru school now and will soon be enjoying your vacation. Do take good care of yourself and Bernice and don't see too much of your friend.

I am homesick for L.A. and wish I were back this minute and you and I were at the beach together, but I am

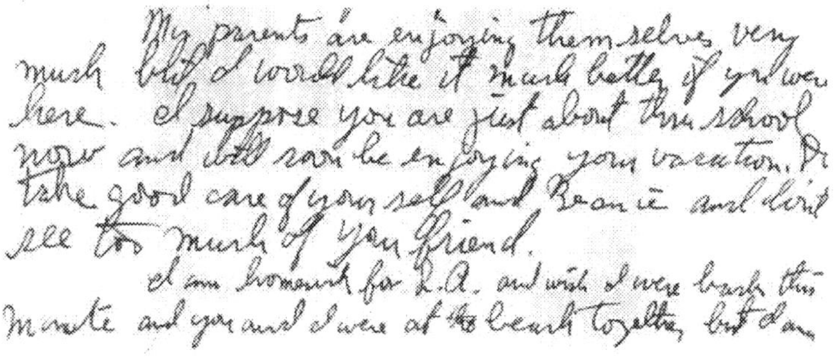

Fig. 30 Tangling lines in the handwriting of J. Paul Getty

Table 8 Line spacing as a measure for reality

	Wide	Narrow	Tangled lines
+	Clear overview, controlled relationships with outside world, talent for organization	Strong bond to environment, directness	Tendency to lose overview, interference, when seen with strong movement: risk of unconscious characteristics getting the upper hand
-	Loss of directness, a loner, social isolation	Lack of distance, need for contact, does not like own company	

Direction of Lines

This involves the direction and form of the baseline. Basically, rising lines are an indicator of optimism and a generally positive mood, whereas falling lines point to pessimism and dejection. Here the baseline is strongly affected by the writer's current mood, with the exception of an extremely rigid baseline, as shown in Fig. 29. In this case the influence of the guiding image plays a key role, revealing the writer's determination in terms of objectives and directions.

The following baselines can be seen:

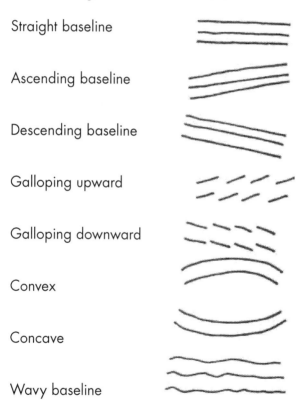

Straight baseline

Ascending baseline

Descending baseline

Galloping upward

Galloping downward

Convex

Concave

Wavy baseline

Fig. 31 Direction of baseline

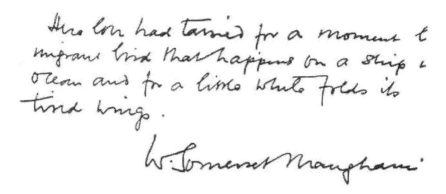

Fig. 33 Slightly wavy lines in the handwriting of Somerset Maugham

Table 9 Direction of lines, attitude toward life

1	Straight: Firmness, determination, consistency, reliability
2	Rising: Impetus, zeal, optimism, buoyancy, possessive, increased impulsivity
3	Descending: Resignation, depression, pessimism, melancholy, possible debility
4	Galloping upward: Conflict between impulse and reason as a countercheck
5	Galloping downward: Fight against despondency and depressive tendencies
6	Convex: A fire that quickly burns itself out, enthusiasm without stamina
7	Concave: Ability to overcome initial reluctance
8	Wavy lines: Changing moods, lack of constancy in attitude toward life, instability, aimless, moody
9	Rigid baseline: Dependency, discipline, feelings of insecurity

Margins

Margins refers to the space left free on the left and right sides of the page. The space left above and below the text is less important to graphology.

The following types of margin can be found:

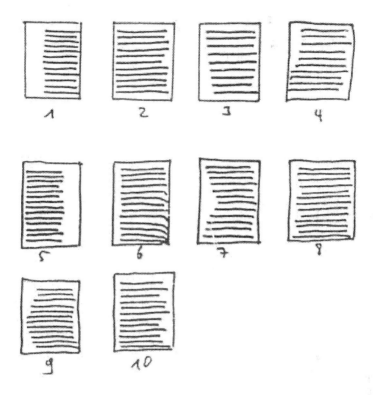

Fig. 34 Types of margin

Margins play a key role in learning about the unconscious character of a writer: those who are thrifty can easily be distinguished from others who are generous or magnanimous. Incidentally, this also applies to the layout used on an envelope.

1. Wide left margin: Generosity, aesthetic sense, feeling for quality
2. Left margin narrow or missing (the width of a thumb is required at the very least to hold a piece of paper in place while writing): Prudence, modesty, economy
3. Increasing left margin: Growing need for communication, enthusiasm, impulsivity

4. Decreasing left margin: Growing restraint and deliberation (a proper left margin basically indicates a writer's concern to keep to the rules)

5. Wide right margin: Inhibition, fear of life, fear of conflict

6. Right margin missing, narrow or lines drooping at end of page: Strong need for communication, dependency on environment, inability to cope with and complete things

7. Left margin changing: Impulses alternating between restraint and release

8. Irregular margins: Alternation between economy and demands

9. Left margin changing: Initial inhibition giving way to drives

10. Irregular right margin: Generosity combined with inhibition, alternation between wastefulness and economy

2. Picture of Movement

Degree of Connection (Continuity)

Schoolchildren are taught so-called joined-up writing: individual letters are joined within each word, and the words themselves remain separate from each other. As the handwriting becomes more mature, each person shows a personal preference regarding the degree of connection. In the past, graphologists used to speak of an "average breath length" of the writing movement, which prompts the writer to lift the pen after connecting three to five letters. This allows the writer to add the dot to an *i*, cross a *t*, and include foreign accents and so on. The movement picture is an indication of the writer's basic vitality, and it is movement that brings the handwriting to life, makes it look unclear, or even destructures it.

If three to five letters are connected, we speak of a medium degree of connection. If fewer than three letters are connected, the writing is described as being disconnected (juxtaposed) (see Fig. 27). Experience has shown that connected writing is faster, with the writer paying less attention to the picture of form.

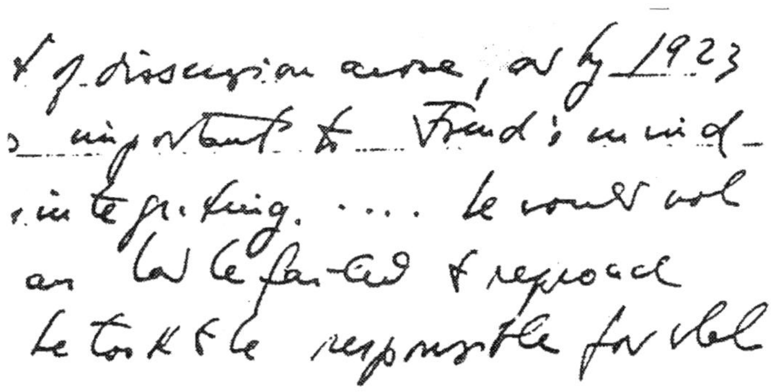

Fig. 35 Connected writing of psychologist Erich Fromm

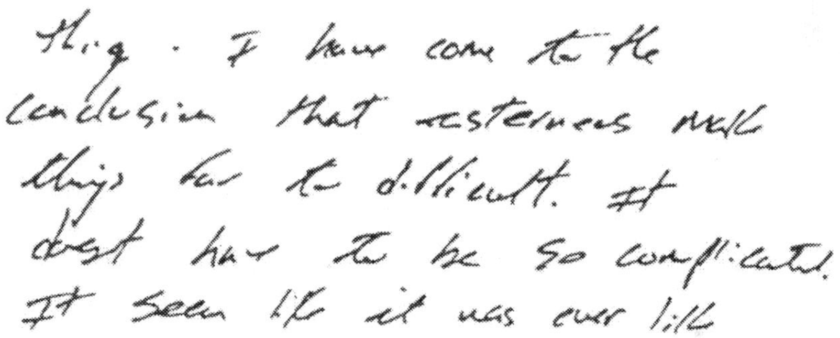

Fig. 36 Unconnected handwriting of a young bank examiner

However, the graphologist is interested not only in whether handwriting is connected, but also in how it is connected. The type of connection is shown in original (creative) connections, shortcuts, and linking of letters toward the right. In Fig. 35 this can clearly be seen in the word *would* in the third line, and also in the first four letters of the name *Freud*. (See also Figs. 11 and 80.)

The handwriting of Erich Fromm includes another special characteristic of connections, so-called *air strokes*. They are produced when the writer lifts the pen from the page, describing a movement in the air to the next letter that can be traced. This increases the degree of connection in a person's handwriting. Look at the word *responsible* in the last line of Fig. 35, in particular the air stroke between the *i* and *b*, and then at the word *failed* in the line above, the connection between the *i*-dot and the next word. This special characteristic can be found only in highly intelligent writers.

To sum it up:

The degree of connection only points toward the way in which a writer absorbs experiences and not to how a writer deals with such experiences.

Table 10 Connection as an expression of coordinated thought

	Connected	Disconnected
+	Logic, deduction, consistency, ability to follow through a sequence of thought, ability to synthesize	Concentration on details, observation, analytical thought, interest in facts, intuition (with rhythmic yet restless writing)
-	Set patterns of thinking, dependency, hasty (depending on letter forms seen)	Flighty, lack of coherence, erratic, inconsistent, disrupted (with disintegrating words)

One special feature in this context is so-called *soldering* (false connections), where the writer is aiming for connection but does not manage to bring it off. With soldering the two parts of the stroke briefly run parallel to each other, as can be seen, where indicated, in the following sample.

Fig. 37 Soldering in a child's handwriting.

Soldering is often a symptom of insecurity—a conscious or unconscious attempt to cover up mistakes or failures. The more frequently soldering occurs in a person's writing and the more disrupted its rhythm, the more negative this interpretation will be.

Special elements:

1. Overconnected: obsessive thought, adherence to ideas and concepts, tendency to escape into ideas

2. Highly disconnected: with major variation in slant, inner agitation, inwardly torn, nervous irritability, inability to adapt

Speed

To assess the speed of a person's handwriting, the graphologist has "to detect in the finished writing picture the dynamics of its generation." Here we assume that all writers have their own basic writing tempo. This also influences the writer's individual maximum speed and speed perceived at a subjective level by the writer. There are handwritings that look very fast yet were in fact written slowly. Writing at a speed that is faster than comfortable can particularly be seen in the handwriting of people who are under great pressure to perform at work.

When interpreting the speed of handwriting, the graphologist must basically consider the following: with mature writing, where the writer has fully mastered the writing process, speed no longer depends on skill, but on the emotional state of mind and temperament.

In terms of performance the writer wants to deliver the most comprehensive result possible in the shortest possible time. The writer can best achieve this objective by taking shortcuts wherever feasible. Graphic features of a high writing speed are shortcuts in the writing path, smooth strokes, simplified forms, small size, width, sometimes disintegration of the form of connection, hasty diacritics such as *i*-dots, foreign accents, and so on.

The following *characteristic elements* point to rapid writing:

> brisk, swift, dynamic, brash, liquid, gliding, lively, expansive, impulsive, turbulent, hasty, hurried, excited, fidgety

The following characteristics can be found in slow writing:

> tired, lame, sluggish, lethargic, weary, creeping, reflective, tentative, not smooth, hesitant, inhibited, uncertain, faltering, fractured, blocked

In graphology the following *features* are traditionally seen as indicators of *haste:* smooth stroke, increasing right slant, progressive, imprecise diacritics (often written like commas), shortcuts, increased degree of connection, strokes and word endings tapering off (wavy movements and threadlike forms), tendency toward width, increasing left margin, ascending lines.

Features pointing toward slow speed: lack of smoothness in stroke, careful attention to detail, precise positioning of diacritics, copybook style, enrichment and decoration, more interruptions, tendency toward narrowness with angular forms, no shortcuts.

Some time ago an empirical study performed in France established additional features by asking 519 people to write the following sentence several times:

Je respire le doux parfum des fleurs.
(*I breathe the sweet fragrance of the flowers.*)[12]

The fastest person wrote at a speed of 249 letters a minute, and the slowest at only 80. It was noted as a basic rule that a large middle zone will slow down the speed of a person's writing.

In the course of the study forty-one script features were taken into account and the following were identified in terms of speed or slowness, listed below in order of importance:

---

12   A. Lombard, D. Prot, and L. Rostand, "Recherche sur la Vitesse" ("Investigation of Speed"), *La Graphologie*, no. 195 (July 1989): 22–32.

Speed

Skillful connections, flowing, dynamic, simplified, rightward tendency, thready forms, irregular, wide, ends of words trailing off, wide word and line spacing, medium pressure, medium tension of stroke.

Slowness

Static, complicated, acquired, print script, narrow writing, short upper and lower lengths, regular, leftward tendency, forms in arcades, disconnected, emphasis on word endings, excessive or insufficient pressure, pasty.

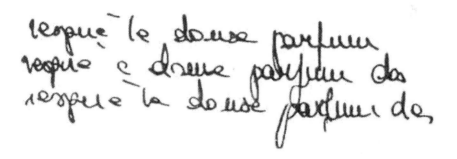

Fig. 38 Slow writing, 120 letters per minute. Features indicating slowness complicated, narrow, leftward tendency, word endings emphasized, heavy pressure, pasty. One indicator of speed: irregular.]

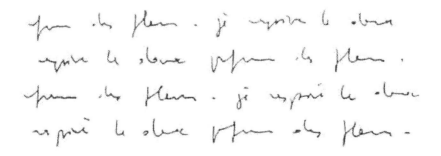

Fig. 39 Rapid writing, 210 letters per minute

Other examples of rapid writing can be found in Figs. 9, 11, and 23, and for slow writing in Figs. 8, 16, and 28.

Table 11 Speed as an expression of the intensity of drives in relation to thought, emotion, and desires

	Rapid writing	**Slow writing**
+	Active, mobile, spontaneous, initiative, lively, open to stimuli, busy, carefree	Reflective, collected, patient, reliable, contemplative, composed, thorough, stable
-	Restless, impatient, changeable, hasty, superficial, rash	Stagnation, immobile, sluggish, taking easy way out, slow, dull, phlegmatic

In this context, one special element is an alternation of writing speed, which points toward an inconsistency of temperament. The writer thus fluctuates between drive and inhibition.

Pressure

Like speed, pressure must also be determined from the finished handwriting. Here heavy pressure applied on the downstrokes will cause the stroke to become wider, and with lighter pressure on the upstroke it will become narrower. If a metal nib is used for writing, the flow of ink can be clearly seen. Modern writing implements such as ballpoint or felt-tip pens make it far more difficult to identify the amount of pressure used. If the writer has chosen a felt pen, it may be because writing with such an implement requires less effort and pressure. It is clear that the writing implement and type of paper used are important: furrows may even be produced on the other side of the page by writers who use heavy pressure.

Writing pressure can also be measured objectively during the act of writing by using a "writing scale." The following figure shows the fluctuations in pressure occurring in two people when writing a specific word.

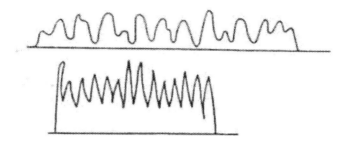

Fig. 40 Different writing pressure is shown by two people.

Pressure, which indicates the intensity of a writer's emotional and psychological development, is an unconscious process. The same applies to major variations in pressure in a person's handwriting. If the pressure is not seen in the downstrokes but on the upstrokes or additional elements of a letter (such as *t*-bars or underlining), we speak of *displaced (deviated) pressure* (Figs. 41, 42). This may ultimately develop into pressure that produces a look of relief on the page—that is, the writing has a "sculpted" effect. To the writer this pressure acts as a guiding image that aims to create an impression of depth (and greater pressure) through demonstrative widening of the stroke.

The feel of the pen on the paper and the writer's feeling of existence and relationship with the page ranges from a feeling of prudence and caution to a strong clash of wills—that is, the writer against the resistance offered by the paper.

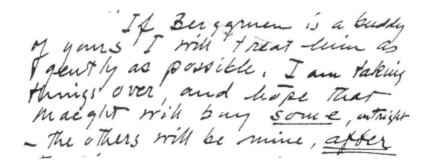

Fig. 41 Strong and displaced pressure characterizes the handwriting of Alexander Calder. The stroke varies in width between upstrokes and downstrokes.

For samples with light pressure, see Figs. 18 and 39.

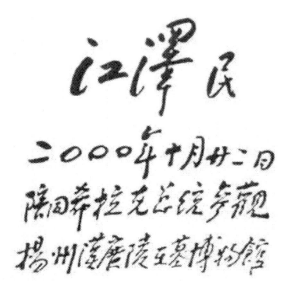

Fig. 42 Pressure displaced onto the horizontal in the handwriting of Jian Zemin, former president of the People's Republic of China

Table 12 Pressure as an expression of the writer's energy

	Heavy pressure	**Light pressure**
+	Vital strength and force, active, insistence, ability to resist, resilience, passion	Adaptability, mobility, skillfulness, sensitivity
-	Hard, robust, inconsiderate, somber	Lack of resistance and force, easily influenced, timid

Special elements:

1. Fluctuating pressure points to an imbalance in the writer's control of energy: tendency to outbursts of emotion, excitability, explosive discharges of energy (Figs. 26, 49)

2. Horizontal pressure or general increase in pressure at end of words: defense against outside world, headstrong, drive toward self-assertion, increasing zeal (Fig. 55)

3. Displaced pressure: forced commitment, strong feeling of mental or emotional tension, engagement

Regularity

Regularity refers to the degree of variation in the individual elements of a person's handwriting. Absolute regularity does not obviously exist in human life, as this would result in stereotyped monotonous letterforms.

There are five main features in handwriting that produce an overall impression of regularity: size, slant, width, baseline, and pressure.

There may also be variation in margins, irregular word spacing, or differences in length, but often just the slant and size of the handwriting are sufficient to create an impression of regularity.

Regularity is assessed by looking at the overall picture made by a person's writing. The majority of the features observed should be regular.

Graphologists see *strength of will* as the guiding image for the regularity of a person's writing. This notion is particularly well expressed by the term *misregulation,* describing the deliberate restraint of an apparently lively temperament. The writing shown in Fig. 43 is typical, and shows both the goal-oriented approach and simultaneous self-control. Such misregulation taken a step further will ultimately result in a strictly disciplined script that is not so much written as drawn.

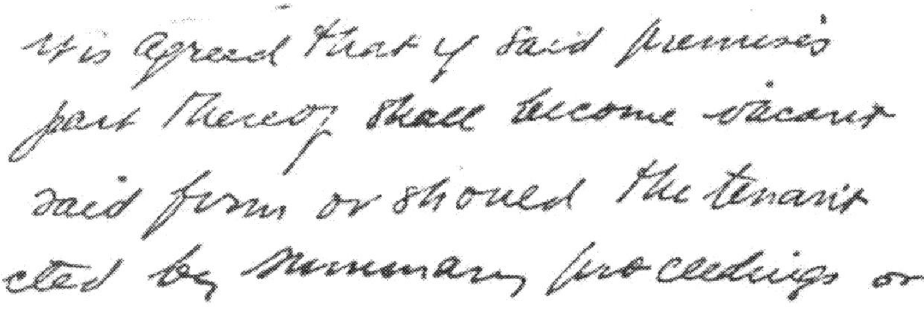

Fig. 43 Regularity of movement

Strictly disciplined script is also described as stylized handwriting in which the writer repeats stereotyped letterforms—in other words, not only is the movement regular, but so is formation of the letters.

Such regularity of movement restricts and hampers the free action of the writing, revealing an increased level of self-discipline, self-control, and a certain self-restraint. Handwriting that reveals a strong drive despite such misregulation (regularity, right slant, width, speed) indicates a very single-minded approach to the writer's objectives (Fig. 43). In a broader sense, people who write in print script also come under this category.

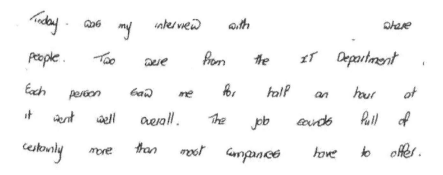

Fig. 44 Regularity of form in a thirty-year-old woman's writing.

In line with the interpretation resulting from the picture of form for a person's handwriting indicating that the writer has a guiding image in mind, we can even speak of an "ethical" regularity—that is, the writer wants to fit in with the rules of society (Fig. 44).

Someone with irregular writing who is either unable or unwilling to write with a regular pattern cannot be seen as capable of adapting, being submissive, or being dominated by will. On the contrary, such a person tends to be a maverick, an individualist who will act impulsively and is unpredictable because of a lack of emotional balance.

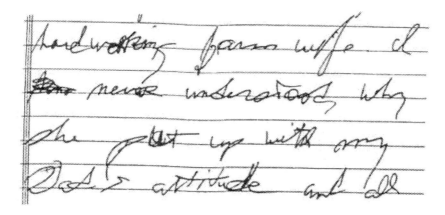

Fig. 45 This irregular handwriting belongs to an American who claimed to be possessed by the devil after taking part in a black-magic ritual at age twelve.

Table 13 Regularity as an indicator for a predominance of will or emotion

	Regular	**Irregular**
+	Discipline, predominance of will, endurance, sense of duty, resistance	Emotionality, spontaneity, impulsivity, passion, openness
−	Tendency to be one-sided, lack of vitality, emotional coldness, person of habit, uniformity	Weak will, inconsistent, moody, lack of consistency, no real direction or objective

Characteristic relationship:

- Regularity of slant = clear strength of will and goal orientation

- Regularity of size in middle zone = stable feeling of self-esteem

- Regularity of width = balanced relationship to outside world

Special elements:

1. Compulsive regularity = one-sided overestimation of will, inability to deal with new experiences because of rigid adherence

to convention and habits, compulsion, tension, neurotic suppression (Fig. 8)

2. Extreme chaotic irregularity = a person is ruled by emotions, moody, tendency of writer to "let himself go," ambiguity, lack of direction, instability, easily distracted

3. Alternation between regularity and irregularity = imbalance between will and emotions, including a closed mind

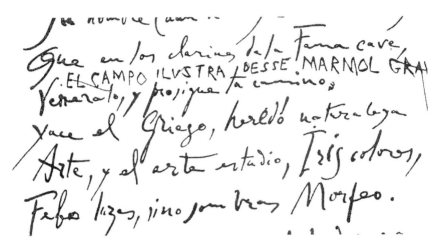

Fig. 46 Irregular handwriting of artist Pablo Picasso

Stroke (Pasty/Precise)

Handwriting graphologists see the stroke as revealing the true substance of a personality, which prompted Pokorny to describe analysis of the stroke as having "basically greater significance for character analysis than most of the other characteristics of handwriting that can be distinguished in terms of morphology."[13] The stroke also plays a key role in judicial graphology, particularly the tension of the stroke and its feeling of assurance. Before the courts, it is generally magnified with the help of a zoom stereo microscope.

---

13 R. Pokorny, *Psychologie der Handschrift*, (Munich: E. Reinhardt, 1968) 146.

The quality of the stroke also plays an important role for autograph-hunters, who see the original trace as representing a person's aura—and often pay a high price for the privilege to own an original.

The stroke tells the graphologist a good deal about the nature of a writer. Poor elasticity of movement represents a lack of flexibility, possibly resulting in inadequate emotional adaptability and lost potential for development.

Graphologists normally assess the stroke from three aspects:

1. From the aspect of *expression* the stroke may seem, for example, well colored or dry, soft or hard, dead and mechanical, vibrant, or delicate and cautious.

2. From the aspect of *movement,* it may seem taut and elastic, slack, painted, congested, or overstretched. It may also look as if there is a sliding or gliding action of the pen, or as if it is boring into the page.

3. From the aspect of the *horizontal outline,* we distinguish between a fine and a wide stroke, between a precise and a pasty, blurred stroke, between a broken and a continuous stroke, and between a slender and a wider stroke.

The categories given above can be extended as desired, depending on the impression made by the stroke. However, an original sample of handwriting must always be available, as photocopies or faxes generally distort the stroke's appearance.

As can easily be seen from the above characteristic features, a stroke that bores into the page, for example, is created with heavy pressure, whereas a slender stroke is produced at a higher speed than the painted stroke.

It should therefore come as no surprise that the graphologist Walter Hegar developed a system consisting of four characteristics: heavy or light pressure, a precise or pasty stroke, type of movement (straight or curved), and speed (rapid or slow). If certain features appear together in a person's handwriting, Hegar interprets them in terms of inner conflict or harmony. For example, slow, pasty, and straight writing with heavy pressure is not considered harmonious, whereas other combinations such as heavy pressure and rapid, pasty and slow, and precise and rapid are seen as compatible with each other.

Other graphologists compare handwriting with melody, and the stroke with the sound forming the basis for the melody. Unfortunately, it is not possible to deal with other aspects involving the stroke here; the relevant literature should be consulted in this regard.[14]

The terms *pasty* and *precise* mentioned above must, however, be explained in greater detail, as they form part of the graphologist's basic terminology. The pasty stroke is wider than normal, has blurred edges, and tends to fill the ovals and loops of letters with ink. This stroke is produced by holding the pen so that it is fairly flat in relation to the paper, and moving it loosely. The writing has a well-nourished stroke as shown in the following figure.

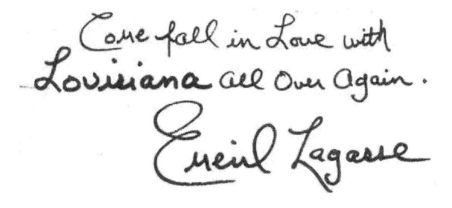

Fig. 47 Pasty writing of American TV chef Emeril Lagasse.

In contrast, holding the pen at a steep angle to the page will produce a fine and precise, taut stroke. There is a marked distinction between the

---

14   E. Dosch, *Graphology of the Stroke* (Canada: IGC, 2004).
Alan Levine, "Die physikalischen Aspekte der Strichstruktur," *Angewandte Graphologie und Persönlichkeitsdiagnosik*, no. 1 (1993): 3–24.
Rudolf Pophal, *Das Strichbild* (Stuttgart: Gg. Thieme, 1950).

edges of the stroke and the white of the page, and the writing is clearly contoured.

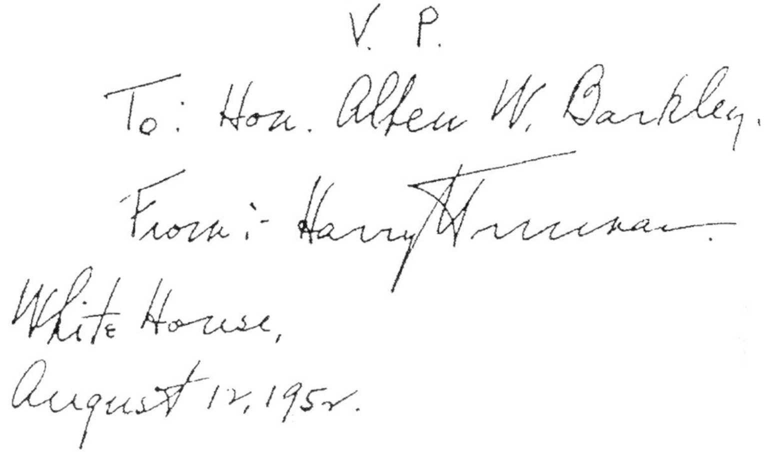

V. P.

To: Hon. Alben W. Barkley.

From: Harry Truman.

White House,

August 12, 1952.

Fig. 48 Precise stroke, t-bars, and ends of words ending in sharp points

A pasty stroke basically indicates an emphasis on the senses, sensuous warmth, and a zest for life. The precise stroke, on the other hand, is an indicator of an intellectual mind and a liking for abstract concepts—but it also shows a lack of physical closeness, someone who has a strict and cold personality.

In the age of felt-tip and ballpoint pens, some graphologists no longer think in terms of *pasty* and *precise,* because the type of stroke produced depends less on the personality of the writer than on the writing implement selected. Although there has undoubtedly been a decline in the importance of this pair of characteristics in recent years, the impression made by the finished script is after all influenced by the choice of implement, as mentioned above. For example, the use of felt-tip pens are sometimes an attempt to impress others, but they are chosen only by writers who are able to express themselves properly with such instruments—that is, people who are happy about the result produced and feel at ease with them.

Table 14 Stroke (pasty/precise) as an expression of human proximity (physical closeness)

	Pasty	**Precise**
+	Zest for life, informal, natural, in touch with the senses	Intellectual mind, shrewd, critical, awareness, tension
-	Lack of control, domination of drives, pleasure seeking, weak resistance	Prosaic, lack of enjoyment, tendency to intellectualize, emotional coldness

Special elements:

1. Excessive pastiness (smeary, blotted): primitive domination of drives

2. Spasmodic pastiness: abrupt sensuousness, possibly ethical guiding image with repressed sensuousness

3. Sharp points (often at ends of words): tendency to criticize, aggressive sarcasm

4. Sharp as crystal: acute mind, intellectual precision (Figs. 26, 48)

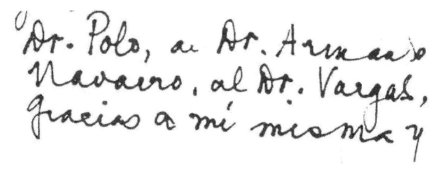

Fig. 49 Pasty spots in the handwriting of Frida Kahlo

Direction of Stroke (Rightward/Leftward)

In European handwritings the direction of movement is from left to right. But to form letters, a writer has to make reverse or left-tending movements as well, and the copybook model therefore contains both right and left-tending strokes.

In the Western world, the rightward direction symbolizes the future, what is new and unknown, the "You," whereas the left represents the past, what is known, the "I" (the ego). In our culture the word *right* has a connotation of what is proper and *left* an association with what is wrong, incorrect, or even underhanded, as used in a large number of expressions.

Handwriting is described as being *right-tending* when (a) strokes tend more toward the right than the school model requires, or (b) when traits that should be leftward according to the copybook tend instead to the right:

(a) (b)

Fig. 50 Right-tending strokes. For (b) see also Fig. 11.

In contrast, a person's handwriting is described as being *left-tending* when (a) strokes tend more toward the left than in the school model or (b)when traits that should be rightward according to the copybook go to the left.

Right-tending script is associated with wide handwriting, whereas left-tending script is linked more to narrow handwriting.

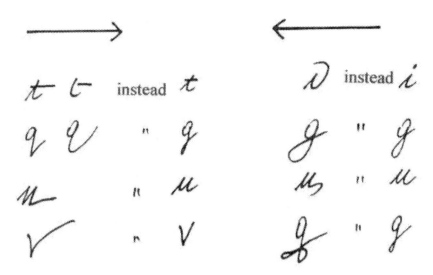

Fig. 51 Particular forms of right- and left-tending handwriting.
(Many other variations are possible.)

Fig. 22 shows left-tending handwriting, and Figs. 32, 36 and 39 are characterized by rightward tendencies.

An overall tendency to the right is the main criterion for extroversion, and a tendency to the left points toward introversion. Generally, little consideration is given to the association between the characteristic direction of the stroke and the bond with the writer's father/mother, which has been observed by graphologists with an understanding of psychoanalysis. Here Pokorny[15] sees a *positive bond* to the father when the upper zone of a person's handwriting shows a marked but not excessive tendency toward the right, that is, *t*-bars with an emphasis to the right or a pronounced right slant of the upper lengths (Fig. 21). A *negative attitude* toward the father is expressed when the upper lengths point to the left. A *positive bond to the mother* is shown by leftward tendencies in the lower zone, for example, with an extended loop of the *g* sweeping to the left, and a *negative fixation on the mother* is shown by rightward tendencies in the lower zone:

---

15 Pokorny, R. "Zur Graphologie des Ödipus-Komplexes." In *Zeitschrift für Menschenkunde*, 26th year (1962), p. 278–288.

the lower loop of the *g* missing, meagerness, and orientation to the right without loops.

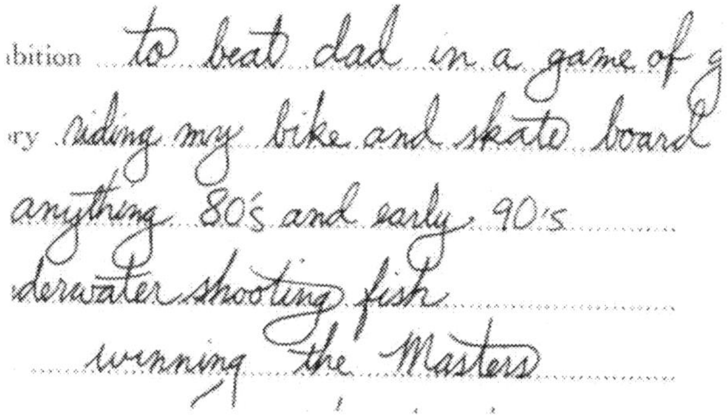

Fig. 52 Strong leftward tendency in upper and lower zone

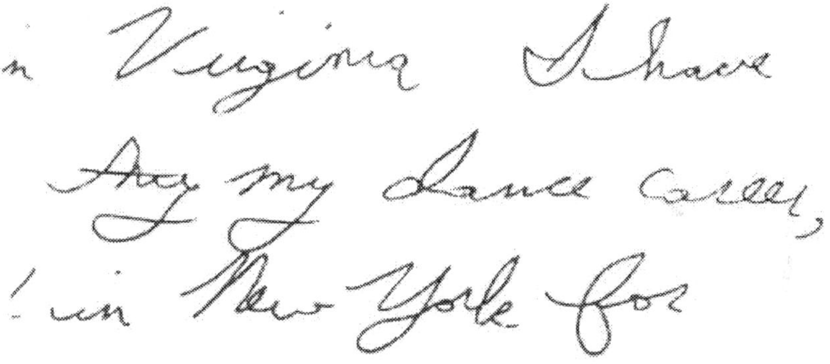

Fig. 53 This example shows a positive bond to the mother.

Table 15 Direction of stroke as an expression for extroversion/introversion

	Right-tending	**Left-tending**
+	Contact with others, need for expansion, willingness to adapt, belief in future, tolerance	Internalization, introspective, looking toward the past, caution
-	Lack of internalization, a "driven" personality, shallow, talkative, continually busy	Egocentric, possessive, difficulties in adapting

Special features of left- and right-tending handwriting in the three zones:

1. Upper lengths tending to the right—for example, incorporating diacritics (Fig. 18) = deduction, logical thought

2. Upper lengths tending to the left (Fig. 10) —for example, the lyrical *d,* something that is frequently found in the handwriting of poets and is a sign of introspection

3. Starting strokes in garlands = pronounced attitude of amiability (Fig. 53)

4. Lower lengths taking the form of a round loop billowing out to the left = well-developed subconscious, sexual fantasies (Fig. 51, line 2)

5. Lower lengths right tending (Fig. 48), forming a sharp angle with the next letter = drives are translated into will and achievements

6. Lower lengths with double loops = desire for tenderness and to be spoiled, vanity (Fig. 51, line 4)

Initial and Final Emphasis

The special diagnostic significance of the beginning and end of a word or line is based on the principle of the focus of attention.

Initial letters are often influenced by conscious impulses toward adaptation, which themselves are shaped by the guiding images held by a writer. Initial emphasis or a lack of it indicates how an individual is positioned in the world and the writer's own perception of this position. Initial emphasis may derive more from an impulse for movement and as such indicate a desire for action and engagement—or it may express a preoccupation with form, something that points to the writer's wish to make an impression and look superior. Extroverted writers generally increase the size of initial letters because they want people to take notice of them.

Final emphasis shows a writer's ability to follow through in terms of achievements or adaptation to the outside world: whether the writer tries to assert his authority, puts up a defense, or adapts to the environment.

Enlarged initial letters can be seen in the handwriting of Picasso (Fig. 46), whereas Fig. 12 shows a tendency toward a reduction in size. An increase in the size of letters at the end of a word can be found in the writing of F. J. Strauss (Fig. 6), and a reduction in Fig. 9. The characteristic features initially observed are important in this context, as they may reveal pride and vanity or a wish to blend into the background or modesty.

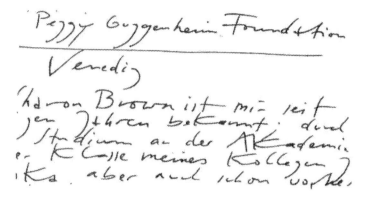

Fig. 54 The accentuated initials in an aesthetically stylized handwriting are those of a professor at an art institute for jewelry design

The handwriting in Fig. 54 shows two typical examples of initial emphasis that can often be found in modern-day writings. First is the long, straight starting stroke (fourth line in the word *und*), which reveals a liking for action and ambition, and is thus also seen by graphologists as an indication of zeal. On the other hand, the emphasis on the initial garlands in *N* and *A* points toward marked amiability in contact with others—that is, when meeting new people for the first time, for example, when working as a sales representative.

Initial letters that are particularly large and also embellished with flourishes indicate a need for recognition, an exaggerated desire to make an impression, and vanity. If the initial letters are especially full and wide, the writer needs plenty of space at the first encounter and may seem overbearing and pompous. How he or she will act in further acquaintance can be seen from the letters in the word that follow.

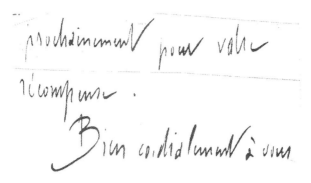

Fig. 55 Enlarged end strokes in the narrow writing of Maurice Ravel

End strokes may be directed upward to the right (Fig. 55) and in unconstrained writing point to ambition. They may trail away into a thread (Fig. 39), indicating that the writer runs out of energy or loses interest, or they may take the form of horizontal strokes. In this last case one possible interpretation is an attitude of defense and a wish to keep one's distance, something that is reinforced and borne out by the left slant. Here the heavy pressure is like a fist held up by the writer to the outside world.

The following question should always be asked: how do the beginning, middle, and end of a word fit together? Is there a change in behavior in the process? The beginning of a word represents how the writer sets about a task, the middle of the word how he or she carries it through, and the end of the word how he or she concludes it or attains the goal.

Table 16 Initial and final emphasis as an expression of self-esteem (form) and an expression of progression (movement)

	Initial emphasis	**Lack/deficiency of initial emphasis**
+	Superiority, pride, wish to impress, élan, pleasure in taking action	Modesty, simplicity, reserve
-	Tendency to be showy, craving to be noticed, megalomania	Uncertainty, anxiety, feeling of inferiority (also with collapsing middle zone)

	Final emphasis	**Lack of final emphasis**
+	Determination to dominate, increase in will, opposition, resistance	Adeptness, tact, diplomacy, adaptation
-	Lack of tact, defense, fanatical determination for self-assertion, unwillingness to see other points of view	Fatigue, easily influenced, weakness

3. Picture of Form

Strength of Form

Strength of form refers to the stability of the forms shown by a person's writing and generally falls between the two extremes of being either rigid or shapeless. If the letters in writing are evenly formed, the stability of form will result from a guiding image that is striving for balance in the life form. Regularity in form reveals a symmetry of the controlling forces acting on a writer—that is, the influence of a constant and balanced will on behavior.

This feature allows us to draw conclusions about the *continuity* of the writer in *coping with life,* his ability to adapt, and the level of predictability in terms of behavior.

The strength of form shown by handwriting specifically reflects a person's inner structure. A harmonious personality will be seen in a rhythmic balance—in other words, in letters falling between the extremes of rigid and of shapeless forms. The following comment was made by the graphologist Thea Stein-Lewinson:

> If an individual allows himself to be constrained to a significant extent in his handwriting, his personality will also be constrained, i.e. he is inhibited by rational control and is unable to attain a rhythmic balance. On the other hand, if the forms in his writing are very shapeless, rational control will be so lacking in such a writer that

he will be unable to control his level of arousal. It is thus apparent that constraint corresponds to unfavorable control inhibiting the writer while shapeless forms stand for relaxation of any control that is equally harmful.[16]

Where strength of form is concerned, we should always consider the question of driving forces. The following combinations are possible:

Form   Drive

1.	Rigid	weak	=	paralyzed form	Fig. 66
		strong	=	compressed form	Fig. 55
2.	Firm	weak	=	genuine form	Fig. 15
		strong	=	stable form	Fig. 24
3.	Mobile	weak	=	loose form	Fig. 12
		strong	=	deft form	Fig. 18
4.	Soft	weak	=	instable form	Figs. 22, 53
		strong	=	fluctuating form	Fig. 28
5.	Shapeless	weak	=	faltering	Figs. 39, 71
		strong	=	flowing	Fig. 36

Table 17 Strength of form as an expression of mental energy

Rigid	Firm	Mobile	Soft	Shapeless
Tension, lack of vitality, little emotional flexibility, immobility, refusal to adapt	Self-control, stability, ability to cope with stress, doggedness	Naturalness, adaptability, emotional flexibility, ability to "go with the flow"	Easily influenced, open to new experiences, emotional dependency	Compliant, changeable, lack of resistance, unpredictability

---

16 T. Stein-Lewinson and Joseph Zubin, *Handwriting Analysis* (New York: King's Crown Press, 1942).

Ampleness of Form: Fullness and Thinness

Depending on the two-dimensional shape given to a person's handwriting, we speak of full or thin script.

The more space the strokes of someone's writing enclose, the more ample and full it will be. It is often the sweeping curves of garlands or arcades that produce an impression of fullness. For example, curved antiqua-style (Latin) handwriting is fuller than German script, which is dominated by angles and straight lines. A full handwriting can be further enriched with flourishes and loops, and a thin script can be simplified or neglected if the writer omits individual elements of letters.

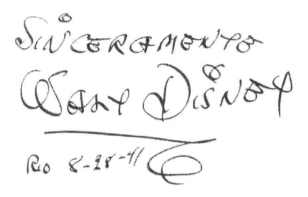

Fig. 57 Walt Disney's handwriting was full and embellished.

The handwritings shown in Fig. 15 and Fig. 48 are categorized as being thin.

When interpreting a person's writing, it should be considered whether the impression of fullness or thinness is created in the upper, middle, or lower zone. A full handwriting generally points to "heart over head."

Basically, a full or ample handwriting indicates breadth of experience, imagination, and creativity, whereas thin writing, in contrast, may stand for a down-to-earth approach, lack of imagination, or a general emphasis on logical thought.

- **Fullness in upper zone**: Imagination, ideals, illusions (with overly inflated forms)

- **Fullness in middle zone**: Wealth of feelings, emotion, a warm heart

- **Fullness in lower zone**: Emphasis on sexually oriented drives

Thinness of forms points to dominance of reason over emotion. The two extremes of imagination and rationality can both appear in a positive or negative manner: imagination can degenerate into illusion and rationality into unimaginativeness. Handwriting of course reveals only *how* the writer thinks, and not *what* the writer thinks—that is, the specific content of his or her thoughts.

Table 18 Fullness and thinness as an expression of emphasis on emotion or reason

	Full handwriting	**Thin handwriting**
+	Fantasy, imagination, human proximity, emotional approach to life	Rationality, objectivity, a sharp mind, abstract thought
−	Subjectivity, inability to think in abstract terms, lack of emotional detachment	Lack of imagination, inner barrenness, feeling of constraint, overrrationalization

Special elements:

1. If upper/lower lengths are fuller than short lengths, general interests are more important than the writer's own affairs.

2. If short lengths are fuller than upper/lower lengths, imagination comes into play more in the writer's personal life

3. Retouched loops indicate a need for clarity; the writer possibly wants to look more imaginative than he or she actually is.

Richness of Form: Enrichment and Simplification

The addition of extra lines and shapes to letters is known as *enrichment*. In extreme cases this results in curlicues and stylization, which is invariably caused by a wish to attract attention.

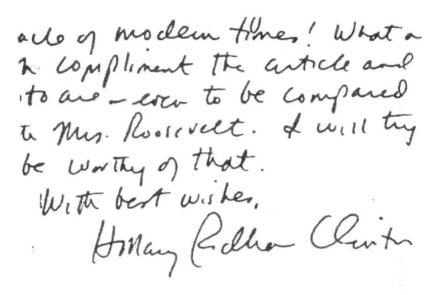

Fig. 58 Simplified handwriting of Hillary Clinton

The form of one's handwriting can then take the other extreme when it is seen as a means to an end. In this case shortened strokes result in a handwriting that has been minimized or pared to the essentials. Here we speak of **simplified** handwriting (Figs. 15, 36), a style that is in line with modern life.

If the writer takes simplification to the extremes, we speak of neglected handwriting (Figs. 32, 39). Here essential parts of a letter are left out because of the brilliance of the writer, his haste, or impatience. This may point to tolerance, idiosyncrasy, and independence. Conversely, it could indicate a lack of consideration, unreliability, a nervous temperament, or possibly intentional ambiguity.

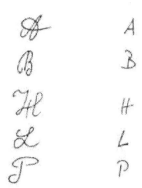

Fig. 59 Enriched and simplified initial letters and one enriched sentence

The school model acts as a benchmark when assessing whether a writer wants to attract attention and make an impression with his enrichments or whether the writer is paring his handwriting down to the essentials by minimizing it. But above all, the forms of the letters should not become ambiguous, thereby making the script more difficult to read.

With enrichment the second step is always to question the extent to which it is appropriate and whether it is truly aesthetic. As in the case of art, eccentricity and mannerisms can result in mere stylization and affectation in handwriting. Each assessment will be decided by the form level of the writing.

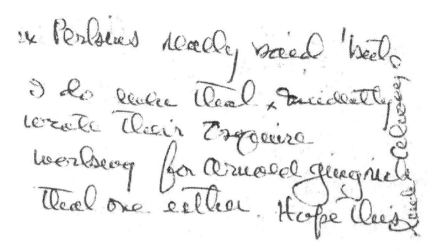

Fig. 60 Full and embellished writing of Ernest Hemingway.
Strong oral tendencies can be seen in his pasty garlands.

Fullness and enrichment reveal a writer's motivating force, but the writer's talent determines whether it is done skillfully, in an original and expressive manner.

Taking both features into consideration, a full and enriched handwriting is typical of the artist, whereas a thin, simplified writing is characteristic of the scientist. The following table simplifies this correlation:

Richness of form	Fullness	Thinness
Enrichment	Artists' handwriting	Nineteenth century
Simplification	Twentieth century	Scientists' handwriting

Table 19 Enrichment and simplification as an emphasis on aesthetics or objectivity

	Enriched handwriting	**Ornate handwriting**
+	Aesthetic drives, a sense of form, delight in variety of life	
-		Trivialization, irrational approach, making "heavy weather" of things, vanity, smugness
	Simplified handwriting	**Neglected handwriting**
+	An eye for the essentials, businesslike, objective, knack for simplification, puritanical	
-		Indifference, lack of consideration, utilitarian approach

Special elements:

1. Touching up, retracing: nervous self-control

2. Missing letters/parts of letters: lack of concentration

3. Idiosyncratic letter formations: tendency to distort the facts

Form of Connection

Within our culture it is normal to connect the letters within each word, and the school copybook specifies how the initial and end strokes are to be formed. However, a whole range of personal variations from the copybook are possible for connecting individual letters.

The entire handwriting can be characterized by certain types of movement, for example, angle, garland, or arcade.

Angle:		Garland:		Arcade:	
Supported:		Supported:		Supported:	
		Looped		Looped	
Thread:		Angular		Angular	
Supported:			Double curve		

Fig. 62 Overview of forms of connection in handwriting

In his book *Handschrift und Charakter,* Klages introduces his interpretation of the form of connection by identifying round forms as organic and angular forms as inorganic.

In handwriting, angles are seen as being relatively firm, decisive, and hard, whereas garlands are flowing, soft, and "connective". When relating the movement to the drive that produced it, the following applies: "The more the drive is exclusively predominated by the image of the goal, the more linear the movement appears to be. Increased movement toward the goal results in increased angular movement. On the other hand, the movement becomes more curved when it follows a need for contact and unity instead of the image of a goal. The straight line is the expression of a targeting and achieving movement of the soul, whereas the curved line represents a more embracing, encompassing movement of the soul"..[17]

In relation to the guiding image, the *garland,* with its emphasis on the upward stroke embodies what is soft, flowing, and open. An elastic and sweeping garland points to a relaxed, natural, and free-and-easy attitude. A "garland writer" is not fond of hard conflict.

The *arcade,* on the other hand, points to a tendency toward concealment, covering, and self-containment. Unlike the garland, it does not look like an open bowl but like a covering arch, something that reveals an ability to cope with stress.

Incidentally, we should avoid the assumption that arcades point to a low level of activity. It is entirely possible to see arcaded writings that are fast, slanted, and wide with tight lines.

---

17   L. Klages, *Handschrift und Charakter* (Bonn: Bouvier, 1956), 107.

The writer of arcades is also someone who tends to suppress his feelings and was brought up to show a "stiff upper lip." A high level of awareness and self-control combined with reserve and formality can likewise be expected from such writers.

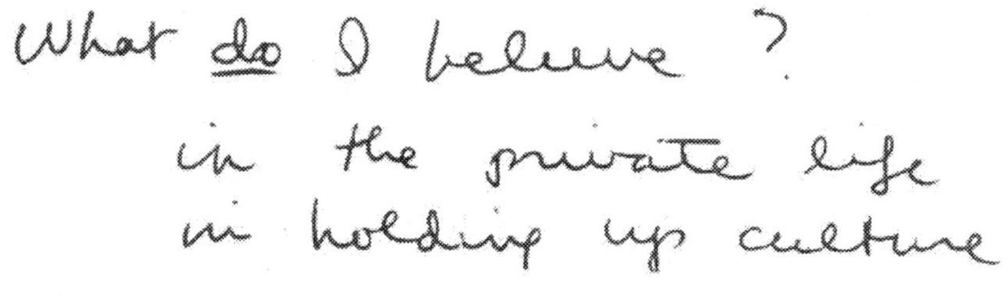

Fig. 63 There are impressive garlands in the handwriting of Susan Sontag.

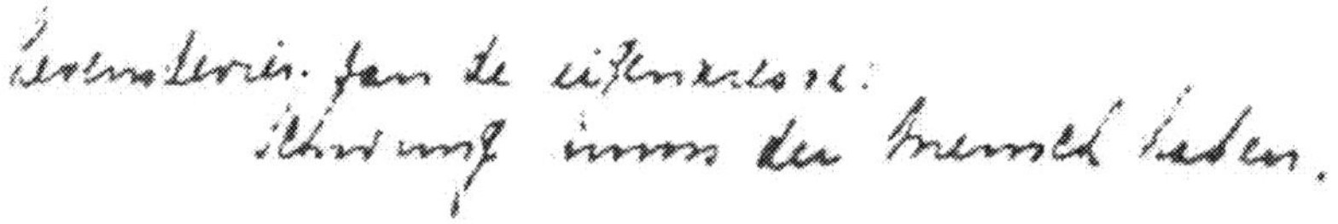

Fig. 64 Arcades are evident in the handwriting of Anne Frank.
The second line reads, 'Schwung muss der Mensch haben.'
The arcade connection in her handwriting is strikingly
symbolic of her concealed situation in Amsterdam.

The straight lines used in the *angle* create an impression of directionality, based on the geometric principle that the straight line and only the straight line is the shortest distance between two points. In the vertical direction the straight line emphasizes strength and possibly rigidity, whereas on the horizontal, it points toward a single-minded drive for assertion.

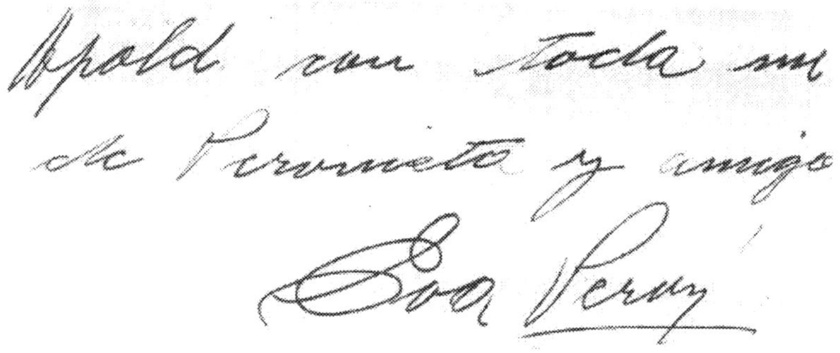

Fig. 65 Angles and a right-leaning slant show
the willpower of Evita Perón.

Examples of angular writings can be found in Figs. 41 and 55. See Fig. 38 for supported garlands, Fig. 60 for looped garlands, and Fig. 75 for looped arcades.

The *thread connection* owes its name to its resemblance to an unraveled thread (Fig. 32). Threadlike (or filiform) handwriting is a loose form that lacks a regular alternation between tension and relaxation. The thread may show light or heavy pressure, with the interpretation being positive for heavy pressure and negative for light.

Here a distinction should be made between the true thread and the so-called hasty thread (Fig. 39), often no more than a straight line between two letters. The hasty thread is frequently seen at the end of words.

Many successful people use the thread connection, with their reluctance to allow themselves to be "nailed down" turning into versatility, dexterity, and diplomacy.

The *double curve* is not seen nearly as often as the thread, and generally appears in weak, unstable handwriting.

Graphologist Steinitzer describes the writer of double curves as someone who does not try to conceal his shortcomings and lack of character as follows: "The most important thing for him is to get through life without bumping into anything. And thanks to his pliant adaptability, he can manage this wonderfully."[18]

---

18 H. Steinitzer, "Die Abreaktion,." *Zeitschrift für Menschenkunde*, no. 3 (1957) 97.

In the handwritings of adolescents the double curve often seems highly artificial, with the writer seemingly putting up a façade. In this case we also speak of so-called "meander writing" that consists of a frozen double curve. This is an indication of inner uncertainty, instability, and lack of force or a striving to fit in as required.

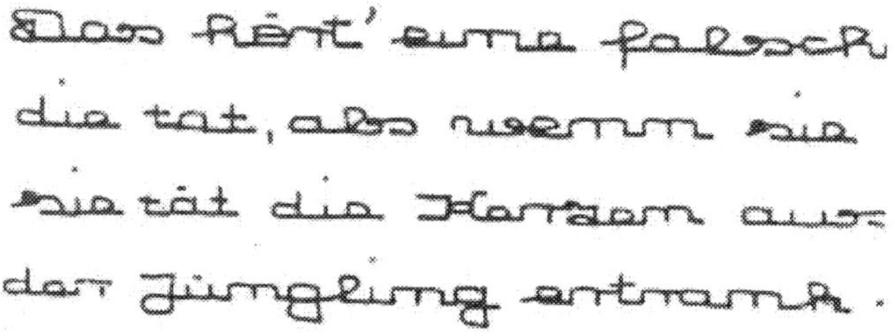

Fig. 66 Artificial square handwriting of a thirteen-year-old girl

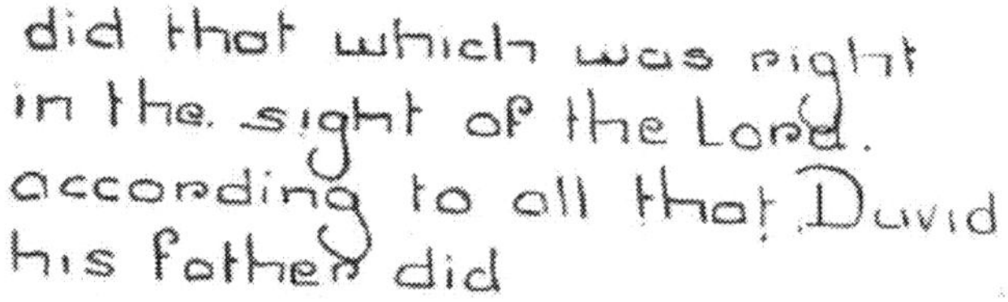

"Meander" or square handwriting of a fourteen-year-old girl

There are also people who prefer mixed forms of connection, thus showing great variation in behavior (Figs. 71, 82). No single form of connection is used here; the writer alternates indiscriminately between all forms of connection, obviously without keeping to any rules. Writers who opt for mixed connections are people who can fully adapt, whatever the situation. They are extremely flexible and always react with ease.

Finally, the copybook form of connection deserves special mention. We speak of copybook handwriting when an adult who is skilled and practiced in writing conforms to all criteria of the school model, particularly in regard to the form of connection. Copybook handwriting among adults points to a strong willingness to submit to the community, to bow to convention and tradition, and to conform to the influence of Freud's superego.

Table 20 Form of connection as an expression of contact with the outside world

	Garland (symbol: open hand)	Arcade (symbol: covering arch)
+	Open, benevolent, empathetic, broad-minded, impressionable, dedicated	Level-headed, self-control, conformity with convention, ability to cope with stress, driven, strong objectivity (with active arcade)
-	Easily influenced, lacking resistance, compliant, taking the "easy way out"	Mistrust, formality, façade, secretive
	Angle (symbol: tension, "black and white" approach)	**Thread (symbol: adaptation)**
+	Decisive, unequivocal, unerring, clarity, reluctance to compromise, strength	Versatility, diplomacy, dexterity, talent for adaptation, ability to improvise, dynamic of innovation (only with heavy pressure)
-	Biased, reluctance to give in, stickler for principles, harsh	Indecisive, no backbone, unreliable, inscrutable

Special elements:

1. Looped garland: calculated amiability, automatic friendliness

2. Supported garland: inhibition, emotional awkwardness

3. Angular arcade: hardness, forced achievement

4. Final thread (hasty thread): empathy, diplomacy, little attention to minor details

5. Double curve: weaving through life, lack of principles and weak character

6. Alternating forms of connection: wide variation in behavior, unwillingness to be nailed down

4

Graphologists have invented a wonderful technique of handwriting analysis and more or less perfected it into an exact science. Although I have neither studied, let alone learned this technique, I have seen its worth proven in many a difficult case.

—Hermann Hesse

Special Questions of Graphology

Psychology of Legibility

With its role of imparting information, handwriting is a means of communication between writer and reader. To fulfill this purpose, writing has to be learned according to a set model and this model then observed as a general standard.

The reasons for the *illegibility* of a person's handwriting may lie with the writer, but also with the reader. It has even been proved that the assessment of legibility varies between different test subjects, from handwriting to handwriting. In extreme cases, however, illegibility is certainly no longer a matter of subjective perception.

Illegibility normally relates to the middle zone of one's handwriting. It may be caused by a general formlessness, deformation of the letters, or an imbalance in the style of handwriting. In addition, the urge to follow a model, which results in "persona" handwriting to mask the writer's true nature, is always taken into account by the handwriting expert.

The graphologist and personnel consultant Kroeber-Keneth has given very detailed consideration to the phenomenon of legibility in terms of handwriting psychology. As legible writing is normally associated with conventions for writing and conventionality in general, the following comment made by Kroeber-Keneth can be easily understood: "People who did not write legibly include Napoleon, Kant, Hegel and Marx. It is not only people of a purely conventional nature who write legibly, but also the great populizers of their age, for example, Franklin or Darwin."

In the literature of graphology, illegibility is not seen as an individual feature of handwriting but as a multilayered phenomenon. It is an indicator of the degree of social consideration shown toward others, guiding images, a need to compensate, and lastly, the maturity of the writer.

Legibility—that is, conforming to the standard—is associated by some authors with a childlike nature and social adaptation in the broadest sense. The graphologist should consider whether a writer's development has been interrupted, and if so, to what extent. In any case, we can always say such a writer wants to make himself or herself understood.

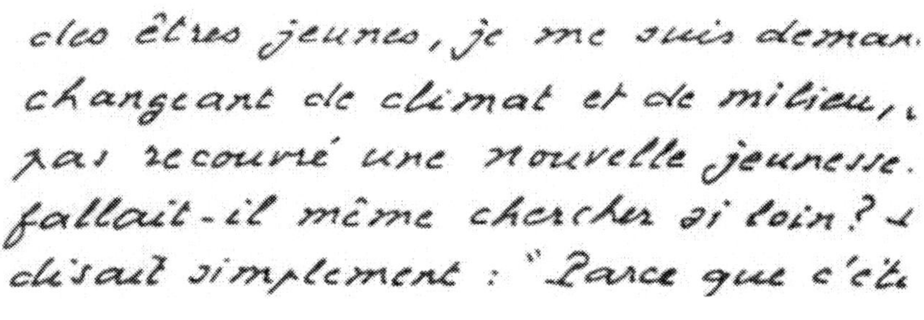

Fig. 67 An extreme example of legibility is shown in the handwriting of a sixty-four-year-old professor of philology.

Experience has shown that the handwriting of those in certain professions, such as bankers and doctors, is characterized by poor legibility. Where prescriptions are involved, the hypothesis has been put forward that a physician is aiming to exclude the patient, either consciously or unconsciously.

Basically, four categories are possible:

1. Being able to write legibly (Fig. 29)

2. Being willing to write legibly (Fig. 67)

3. Not being able to write legibly (Figs. 68, 69)

4. Not being willing to write legibly (Figs. 70, 75)

Illegible writing is seen among artists, and sometimes also in unconventional characters whose inner life is so strongly developed that they completely lose sight of the world around them.

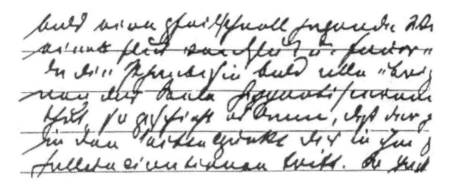

Fig. 68 The famous graphologist Ludwig Klages at age eighteen was an example of someone unable to write legibly.

The handwriting impression has a strong emphasis on movement, with the letters becoming shapeless, as can be seen in the writing of the letters s below.

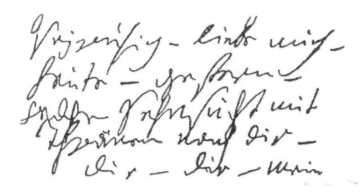

Fig. 69 The handwriting of Beethoven is an example of illegibility.

Not being willing to write legibly, because the writer expects others to make the effort to read his writing, can be seen in the following example. The horizontal tension in the script indicates that the writer's awareness, in Fig. 70, is higher than that of the person with the handwriting of Fig. 71. That writing looks less disciplined and more spontaneous than the script shown in Fig. 70.

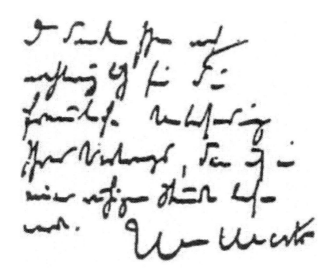

Fig. 70 A fifty-year-old founder and managing director of a company provides an example of not being willing to write legibly.

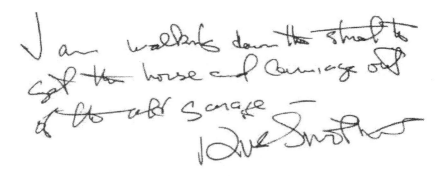

Fig. 71 A race-car driver is not able to write legibly.

Table 21 Legibility as an expression of social consideration

Legibility may point to	Illegibility may point to
a striving for clarity, the wish to be understood, and adaptation or concealment behind the mask of an honest man	genuine or affected idiosyncrasy, lack of social consideration, thoughtlessness, making demands on others, complexity, inscrutability, and unpredictability

The relevant form level will decide what interpretation is chosen in each case.

The Signature as an Expression of Personality

The signature can be seen as the concentrated essence of a writer's overall self-esteem, giving expression to guiding images that may be appropriate or not in each case. Precise analysis of the signature is particularly important whenever there is an emphasis on integration, cooperation, or objectivity.

Changes in the signature in the course of time are especially common in the case of politicians. Well-known examples in this context are the handwriting of Napoleon, Adolf Hitler, and Richard Nixon.

In graphology, the signature has special status because of the legally binding obligation that results. For the purpose of authenticity, it does not have to be legible but uniformly constant. It often lags behind the level of development shown by the rest of one's handwriting, or the writer may have two signatures, one for work and one for his private life. It serves as a "billboard" to a certain extent, particularly in the case of high-profile characters, offering them scope to express all their personal vanities and the desire to make an impression. In the signature the personality presents itself as it would like to be. Here the writer's need for admiration, dreams, and wishes are all laid bare, along with his tendency toward honesty and degree of inner maturity.

The graphologist Max Pulver commented, "In so far as feeling of self can be considered the key to character, the signature can thus mean more than a social sign and an autobiographical sketch—it can lay bare essential signs of the individual's mental structure. Thus it can be either persona, that is to say, a mask or mouthpiece for something hidden behind it—or personality in the genuine sense, the adequate expression of the individual's existential quality."[19]

Basically it should be decided whether the signature differs from the writer's normal handwriting—that is, whether the face that the writer wears in private life corresponds to the one he or she presents to the outside world.

From the above, it can be seen that a signature by itself cannot reveal very much about the true nature of a personality. Particularly in today's business correspondence, we increasingly observe illegible and highly distorted signatures that seem to have no relation to the name in question. This can be interpreted as an identity that does not sit well with the writer, a feeling of anxiety and need for protection. The writer is reluctant to commit himself or herself in moral terms and refuses to accept responsibility.

Sometimes a married woman emphasizes her first name over her married name by writing it more clearly, applying greater pressure or increasing the size. Subconsciously, she still feels like Chris, Liz, or Sue and accentuates the name she had in her childhood and adolescence.

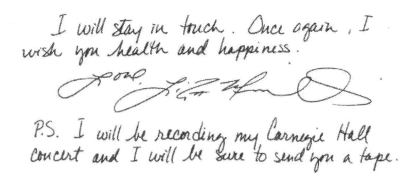

Fig. 72 Liza Minnelli's signature differs from her daily handwriting.

---

19   M. Pulver, *The Symbolism of Handwriting* (London:Scriptor, 1994).

Basically, we can say the following: the greater the similarity between the writer's signature and normal handwriting, the more simple and genuine the writer's nature will be, and the more likely he or she is to have moral courage and integrity.

With indecipherable signatures, the writer is instinctively trying to free himself or herself of an overwhelming feeling of responsibility. Here we should also take the following factors into account: the length of the name, the nationality of the writer, and the speed at which the signature was written.

Other special characteristics seen in signatures such as left-tending extensions in the handwriting of older people, ascending or descending words, retracing, underlining, deletions, and encircling of the signature can be interpreted according to the same principles that are applied to the rest of the text.

Fig. 73 First name legible, last name illegible

The Russian politician in Fig. 75 is not willing to write legibly in his signature, which signifies inscrutability.

Fig. 74 First name and family name are connected; private and professional life are intertwined. The signatures belong to the Italian filmmaker Franco Zeffirelli and to Frank Lloyd Wright. See also Figs. 33, 71, and 94.

Fig. 75 Looped arcades characterize the signature of Vladimir Putin. His handwriting and signature are different from each other. Putin worked for the KGB in East Germany for many years.

Print Script: A Handicap to Analysis

Traditionally, graphological analysis is based on a sample of so-called cursive (joined-up) writing. If the sample has been written in print script, the graphologist often feels that the writing has been depersonalized and is therefore more difficult to analyze.

In recent years the use of print script seems to have become more common, particularly among the younger generation, with the justification that it improves both speed and legibility, a particular claim of left-handed writers.

The graphologist Patricia Siegel examined 175 samples of handwriting submitted in the USA as applications for a job vacancy and observed that 26 percent of women and 40 percent of men had used print script.[20]

In the USA, the use of print script is even more widespread in the lowest grades at school. American culture, which is shaped by immigrants from many different nations, seems to emphasize the clarity of communication in handwriting and not how writing is actually produced. Print script has been taught in the United States since about the beginning of the 1970s. This means that today's younger generation of teachers is unable to write cursive. Consequently, many scripts now show a poor management of space, unsatisfactory legibility, and a lack of fluidity.

Here it is interesting to note that Chinese immigrants often write cursive in the United States because they apparently acquired their basic skills in writing European characters outside America.

In her book *The Pleasure of Writing Cursive*, the Canadian graphologist Graziella Pettinati gives numerous examples of how quickly children can master cursive writing (Fig. 77). In Germany, for instance, teachers are using a simplified method of writing in which many left-tending strokes have been eliminated to increase writing speed. In addition,

---

20 P. Siegel, "Le Script American," *La Graphologie,* no. 228 (October 1997): 119–136.

the basic form of numerous letters has been provided with end strokes tending to the right to make it easier for pupils to learn cursive writing later on.

Basically the use of print script makes analysis far more difficult for the graphologist, who is compelled to concentrate more on global rather than individual features, something that calls for an enormous amount of experience. Here we should mention an emphasis on form or movement, rhythm, drive, and control in handwriting.

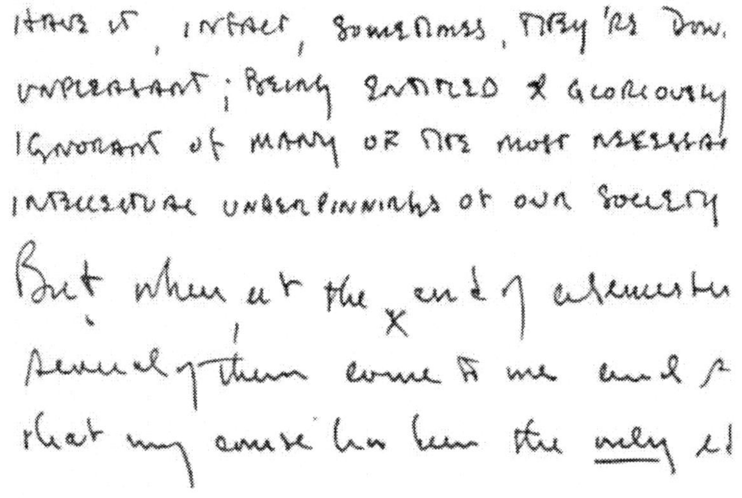

Fig. 76 This sample of handwriting in print script and cursive was produced by a sixty-year-old American writer with a highly idiosyncratic character.

If the graphologist then manages to obtain a sample written in the cursive style, it may look far more childish and undeveloped than the sample in print script. This may in fact be the reason why adolescents from age sixteen mainly use print script. In consequence, this style of writing continues to develop during the writer's life, whereas his "joined-up" writing remains frozen at the level of a sixteen-year-old.

Investigating the graphology of print script would unfortunately go beyond the scope of this book, and readers with an interest in this area should consult the relevant literature. Nevertheless, this is a field with which the professional graphologist should be acquainted.[21]

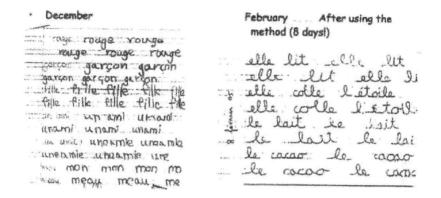

Fig. 77 The handwriting of a six-year-old girl before
and after the training by a graphotherapist

The sample in print script shown in Fig. 44 is noteworthy for its narrowness, wide spacing, and plain forms.

---

21   D. S. Anthony, "Print Script Analysis," *Journal of the American Society of Professional Graphologists* (1989): 28–39.
E. Dosch, "Die graphologische Deutung der Druckschrift," *Angewandte Graphologie und Persönlichkeitsdiagnosik*, no. 2 (1992): 3–31.
M. Steiner, "Entzieht sich die Druckschrift einer graphologischen Interpretation?,"
(degree paper submitted to Zurich: Schweizerische Graphologische Gesellschaft, 1982).

5

Graphology is not only for practicing. In fact, this is its most vulgar task. Graphology is for learning, for opening the mind and the soul. It is for increasing understanding, compassion and tolerance. First and foremost, graphology should be for the graphologist's own education and growth and only through this, for the benefit of humanity.

—Renna Nezos

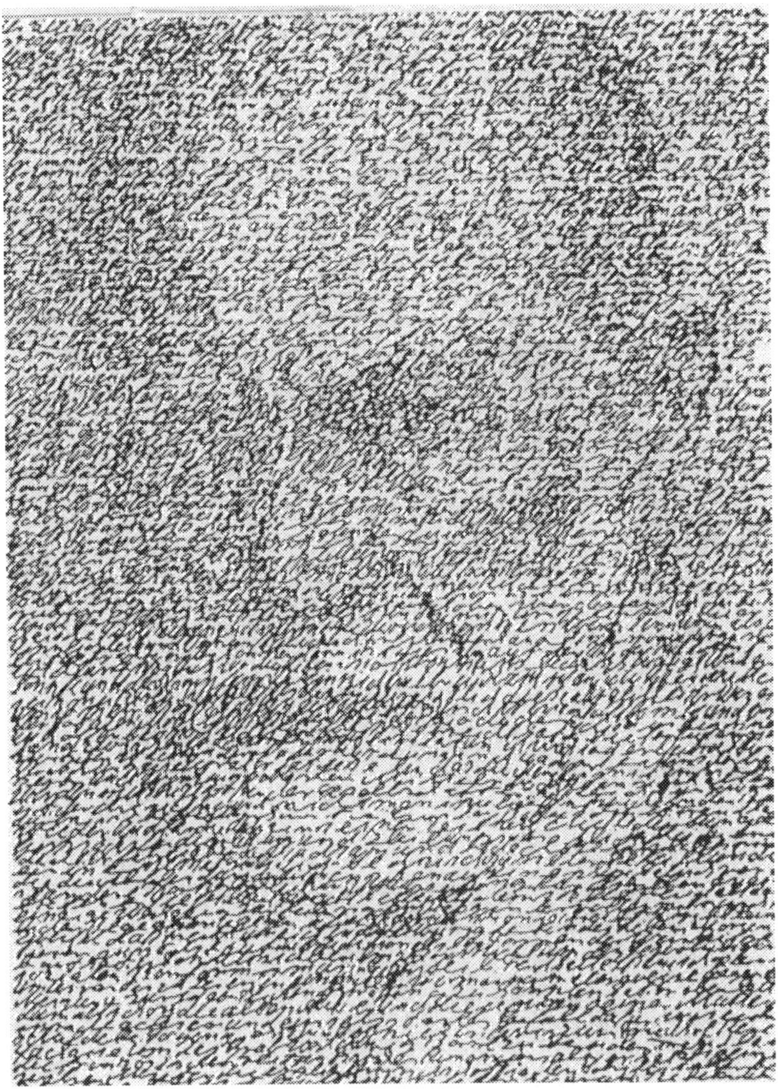

Special Questions

The Question of Intelligence

Although graphologists are repeatedly asked in their work to comment about the intelligence of a writer as it relates to job applications, there are very few publications devoted to this subject. The leading work in this regard written in German is Max Pulver's "Intelligenz im Schriftausdruck" (Zurich, 1949) and in French, Michael de Grave's "La pensée et l'intelligence" (Brussels, 1992). A thesis paper written by Elisabeth Keiser-Gröber at Zurich's Seminar for Applied Psychology deals with emotional intelligence as expressed in handwriting (Zurich, 1996).

The Spanish graphologist Jaime Tutusaus sums up this question as follows: "Intelligence is the ability to see and to grasp the connection between two conscious ideas, to think rationally, to establish efficient relationships with the outside world, to think and act in a methodical manner in order to cope with new problems."[22]

In psychology the aspect of cognitive interaction is also given as a category to describe a personality. The term *cognitive* refers to the acquisition of knowledge by means of mental activity—in other words, conscious thought. Thus, this involves the conscious, rational, or intellectual interaction between the individual and his environment.

22 J. Tutusaus, "Qualitative Intelligence and Its Graphic Expression," *Graphology*, no. 30 (October 1994): 33.

According to graphologist Furrer,

> Cognitive processes start with the perception of information from the environment, with such information being processed by analytical and abstract thinking. The cognitive content of the consciousness (thought) can then be linked up by deductive skills, with the ability to form ideas resulting in new thoughts or concepts. Cognitive content can be imparted to the environment through the ability to communicate. In addition, the individual is able to store cognitive content in the short term by making a mental note and in the long term by using the memory. Ultimately, all cognitive processes come to an end in time, at different speeds.[23]

In the course of the research into intelligence done to date, researchers have not managed to agree on a uniform concept to establish the nature and structures of intelligence to be quantified on an empirical basis. Anglo-American psychology therefore no longer speaks of "intelligence" but only of "factors," which correlate with each other and play a role in intelligence.

The successful use of intelligence, however, involves other personality factors such as an interest in the subject at hand, persistence, self-confidence, identification with a specific task, and so on.

We distinguish between the following:

Intelligence functions (according to Pulver)

- performance in terms of understanding in general

- performance in terms of organization

- performance in terms of goal-oriented consideration

- performance in terms of abstraction

- performance in terms of intensity and concentration

---

23 M. Furrer, *Persönlichkeit und Handschrift*, (Bülach, Switzerland: R. Schmid, 1990), 22.

Orientations of intelligence

- practical (Fig. 94) or theoretical (Fig. 78)

- analytical (Fig. 67) or synthetic (Fig. 80)

- concrete (Fig. 94) or abstract (Fig. 78)

- fluid (Fig. 80) or crystallized intelligence (Fig. 10)

Types of intelligence (depending on the main quality)

- based on intuition (Fig, 80)

- based on creativity (Figs. 46, 54, 57)

- based on criticism (Figs. 26, 55)

- based on interpretation (Fig. 18)

- based on reporting (Fig. 52)

- based on reproduction (Fig. 19)

It goes without saying that the result of the thought process also depends on the manner of perception—in other words, how information is assimilated.

The professional graphologist is capable of making a diagnosis of the functions, orientations, and types of intelligence listed above from the handwriting.

To simplify, a distinction can be made between three aspects:

Striving for clarity

a clear, structured handwriting that has been purposefully simplified

Type of thinking

connected or disconnected handwriting (possibly air strokes)

Skill in making judgments

individualistic and original letterforms

The following may appear as secondary characteristics of intelligence in handwriting:

- easy and fluid movement

- control as a component of will in the thought process

- strong inherent tension of the stroke, which stands for the intensity of intellectual processing and engagement, and possibly pressure displaced into the horizontal

- sensitivity of the stroke as a criterion for intellectuality

- original connections that save the writer time (Fig. 80)

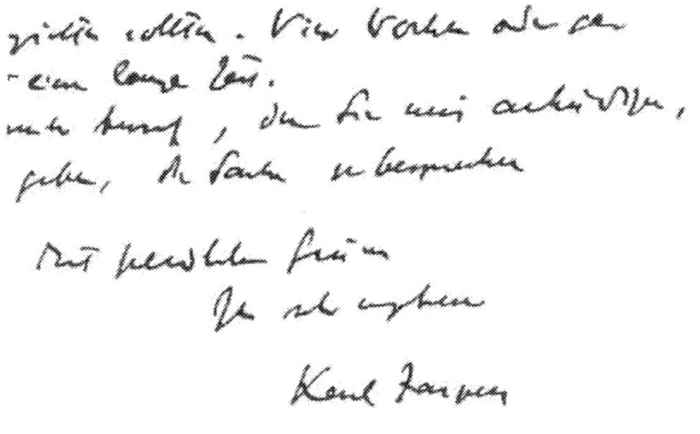

Fig. 78 The handwriting of the philosopher
Karl Jaspers at age eighty-three

The handwriting of Karl Jaspers is a prime example of high abstract intelligence. The letterforms have been simplified to the limits of legibility and are also highly connected and very original.

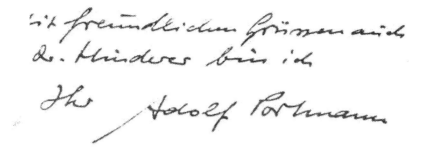

Fig. 79 The handwriting of biologist Adolf Portmann

In the handwriting of this biologist, we can observe the strong element of will in his thought processes, which is indicated by the angles and uniform right slant.

Spinoza cites intuition as the highest form of cognition. In general, intuitive perception or insight comes about suddenly, which normally results in an illuminating realization. Intuition is also known as the "voice of the cosmos" in man. In handwriting the following features point to intuition: a rhythmic handwriting tending toward disconnection, a sensitive stroke, and minor variations in the middle zone indicating individuality, that is, not copybook. Intuition loosens and relaxes the structure of handwriting, and gives life and rhythm to the movement.

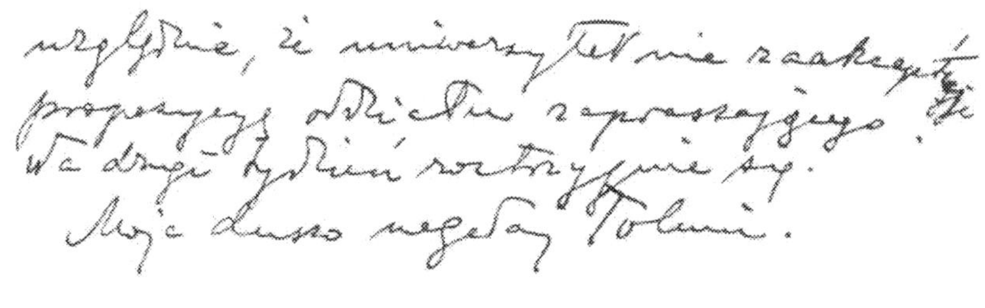

Fig. 80 Intuition in the handwriting of Helene Deutsch,
a psychoanalyst and coworker of Sigmund Freud

The handwriting in Fig. 30 also shows intuition.

Dr. Helmut Ploog

The Question of Honesty

Many clients, such as companies who wish to recruit applicants, ask a graphologist about the honesty, reliability, and conformity of a writer. This entails behavioral patterns vis-à-vis the environment that themselves depend on highly complex circumstances.

On the one hand, the question of honesty involves values and standards held by society that may well vary, depending on the geographical location and morals of the age. On the other hand, dishonesty may be prompted by a wide range of motivations. For example, people may bend the truth to play their cards close to their chest, or through weakness or fear, or because the borders between fantasy and reality have become blurred. But people may also lie from a lack of confidence or intentionally for personal advantage. Dishonesty is often the result of forced attitudes that have become a habit and reveal an effort to adapt that has not yet been mastered.

The graphologist, who as a beginner has to exercise utmost care in his analyses, can consult the so-called signs of insincerity that are dealt with extensively in the literature, preferably practicing on cases personally known to him or her. However, the graphologist will then note that the handwriting of fraudsters, for example, often looks highly conformist. This is of course to camouflage their activities in the business world, which frequently remain undiscovered for a considerable time. In particular, we should also remember the tolerance shown to unstable employees within a company.

As a basic principle, the form level and in particular, the rhythm of one's handwriting will determine whether a negative interpretation is appropriate. However, this calls for a good deal of experience.

Reliability means consistent thinking, feeling, and acting as well as the ability to resist internal and external disruptions. In graphological terms this can be seen in the following:

- homogeneity or uniformity—in other words the degree of balance between all elements of the handwriting or in its harmony;

- the stability of the writing—in other words the relative consistency of the picture of form, which reveals the guiding principles and a person's consistent mind-set.

The characteristics listed below should be seen as warning signs. Many writers want to pull the wool over the eyes of others by distorting the forms of their letters.

Signs of insincerity:

- general monotony of a person's handwriting

- combination of sham, exaggeration, and lack of uniformity, exaggerated loops and spirals (so-called "liar's knots")

- ornate handwriting, print script, and artificial handwriting acting as a mask

- imprecise forms of connection, threads, absence of pressure, conscious or unconscious ambiguity

- substitution and/or omission of key parts of a letter with a writing speed that is otherwise slow

- covering strokes

- soldering in the sense of "covering up the joins"

- frequent retouching or amendments—that is, corrections made because of the writer's feeling of insecurity

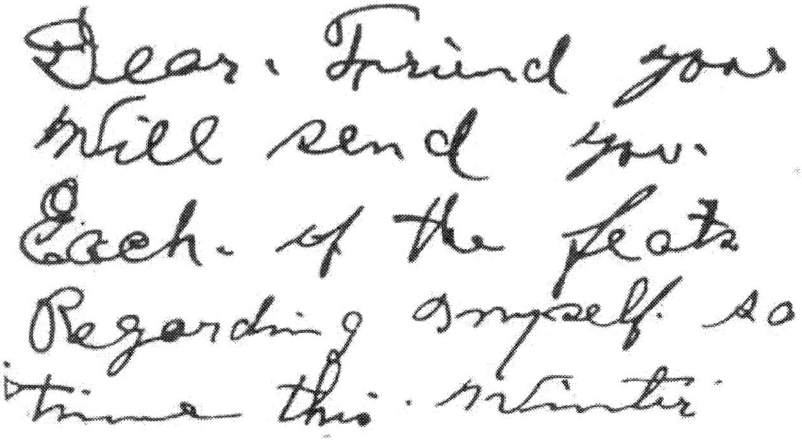

Fig. 81 Covering strokes, circular spirals and touching up

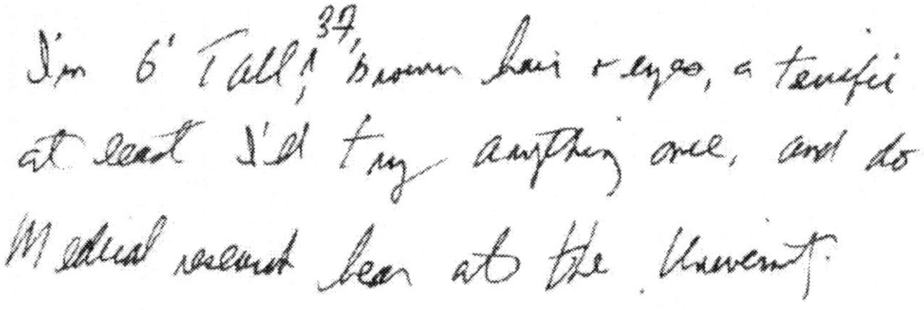

Fig. 82 Disturbed rhythm of movement and distorted letters show a lack of self-control and unpredictable behavior.

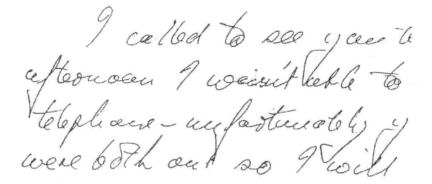

Fig. 83 The many spirals in this handwriting of a financial investment adviser show his very personal interpretation of truth.

In practice no case is alike.

The Use of Graphology in Psychotherapy

Erhard Bertele, president of the Swiss Society for Psychotherapy, made the following comment:

> Time and time again it is astonishing how much the analysis of a good graphologist turns out to be correct. Specific experience with graphology has shown me that in handwriting it is possible to discover information which is also important for psychotherapy, for example the way in which a writer reins in his vitality, spontaneity, creativity and love, where and how he denies his true tendencies and where this is particularly marked in his life. Not lastly, it is also interesting to observe the possibility (extensively developed by graphology) of identifying the writer's relationship to other people, a partner, his environment, his dealings with objects or his work.[24]

24 E. Bertele, "Der Psychotherapeut und die Graphologie," *Angewandte Graphologie und Charakterkunde, no. 3* (1986): 3–5.

If the handwriting of parents or the key people in the writer's environment are also consulted for the purpose of comparison, it will be easier to spot patterns of behavior that go back to childhood bonds, dependencies, complemental attitudes, identification with parents, complexes involving a parent, and so on.

The graphologist is directly presented with a true picture of illness or suffering thanks to his overall view of the situation. Unlike the psychotherapist, the graphologist can at once see from the writing many factors that are relevant to treatment. He or she is also able to identify associations that are often wrongly perceived by the patient or intentionally concealed. The graphologist can observe patterns of behavior that are not appropriate and even diagnose distorted perceptions of reality. However, unlike the psychotherapist, the graphologist is not generally fully qualified for this purpose and runs the risk of encroaching on a field of which he or she knows too little. If treatment is successful, the graphologist will of course notice changes: handwriting that looks fuller and warmer and shows an improvement in movement or fluidity.

Through the writing, it is possible, for example, to see abilities that according to Anna Freud are necessary for successful psychoanalysis, such as the ability to verbalize without disruptions in thought, flexibility, a low tolerance for frustration, and so on. The graphologist Curt Donig points out that if a patient refuses graphological analysis before treatment, it must be expected that attitudes blocking psychoanalysis will not be identified. In addition, patients who are not suitable for psychoanalytic treatment will feel burdened by an intensification of their neurotic symptoms or forced to end treatment prematurely. Clinical experience has shown that there are patients who respond well to psychoanalysis and others who do better with behavioral therapy. This in no way implies any judgment of different types of therapy, just an acknowledgment that graphologists have a reliable instrument allowing them to say which therapy is suitable for which patient.

Although graphology goes back a hundred years, the possibilities it offers for supporting therapy are to date largely unknown among the professionals in this field. Here it may well be the case that psychotherapists do not wish to be provided with advance information from graphology in order to make sure that they are not distracted from the internal principles of the analytical process.

The following examples show how handwriting can be used to check the success of therapy by revealing a change in a patient's essential personality structure. The effectiveness and limits of therapy become apparent here.

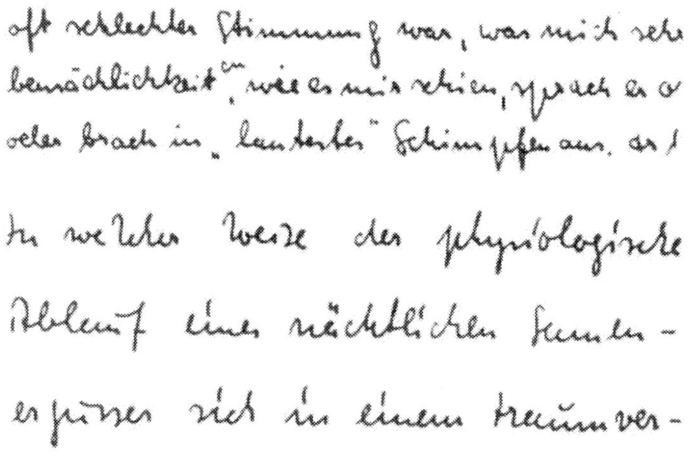

Fig. 84 The handwriting of a twenty-three-year-old skilled tradesman before and after therapy lasting one year

The first example in Fig. 84 reveals inner uncertainty, suppressed aggression, and bottled-up drives. In the second sample, the entire handwriting sample seems to have unfolded and became more open. Movements look freer, more fluid, and buoyant.[25]

A similar positive development after psychoanalysis lasting four years can be seen in Figs. 85 and 86.

---

25 Example taken from dissertation of Arie Naftali: "Die Pophalischen Spannungsstufen der Schrift als Indikator des Heilerfolges in der Psychosomatischen Medizin." Hamburg University, 1959.

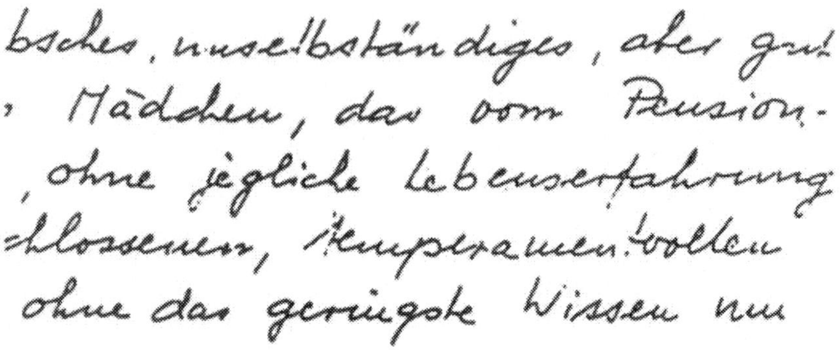

Fig. 85 This handwriting sample is from a teacher,
age thirty-one, at the start of psychoanalysis.

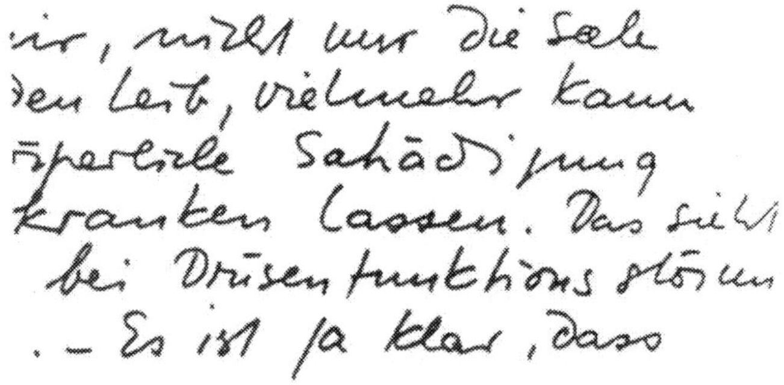

Fig. 86 This writing is from the same person at age
thirty-five, on completion of psychoanalysis.

The second handwriting sample looks far more rhythmic and
individualized, creating a more vital impression through the change
in stroke.[26] This example backs up the hypothesis that the vitality of
a person appears only if comparisons are made between samples of
handwriting.

Other interesting examples of changes seen in handwriting during
psychoanalysis can be found in the works of Teillard.[27]

See also Fig. 93.

---

26 U. Imoberdorf, "Zur Diagnostik von Handschriften und Schriftentwicklung,"
Psychodiagnostik heute, (Stuttgart: Hirzel, 1992), 70–71.

27 A. Teillard, *Handschriftendeutung*, (Bern and Munich: Francke, 1963), 54ff.

In summary, after therapy handwriting may develop in two possible directions:

1. A monotonous and lifeless script starts to loosen up and become more lively during therapy.

2. An extremely stiff and tense writing becomes increasingly relaxed, pointing to easier adaptation on the part of the writer or an absence of conflict in his behavior.

Handwriting of Twins

For a long time graphologists were unable to understand why twins who look so similar have such different handwriting. Klara Roman-Goldzieher undertook an initial study in 1945, as detailed in her book *Untersuchung der Schrift und des Schreibens von 283 Zwillingspaaren.*[28] In this work investigating the handwriting of 283 pairs of twins, she distinguished between identical twins with the same genetic makeup and nonidentical twins whose genes differ. The result was that more than half of the identical twins had similar handwritings, and just over a third of the nonidentical twins.

Pairs of scripts	Identical twins	Nonidentical twins
Dissimilar	25.5 percent	54.5 percent
Similar	57.5 percent	38.0 percent
Doppelgänger script	15.0 percent	7.5 percent

The term *doppelgänger script* is used to describe handwritings that can be barely told apart. The pairs of scripts (113 identical, 160 nonidentical) were rated on a scale consisting of the following four categories:

very similar – similar – dissimilar – very dissimilar

---

28   Klara Roman-Goldzieher, "Untersuchung der Schrift und des Schreibens von 283 Zwillingspaaren," *Graphologia I*, (Bern, 1945).

The next figure shows an example of two similar handwritings.

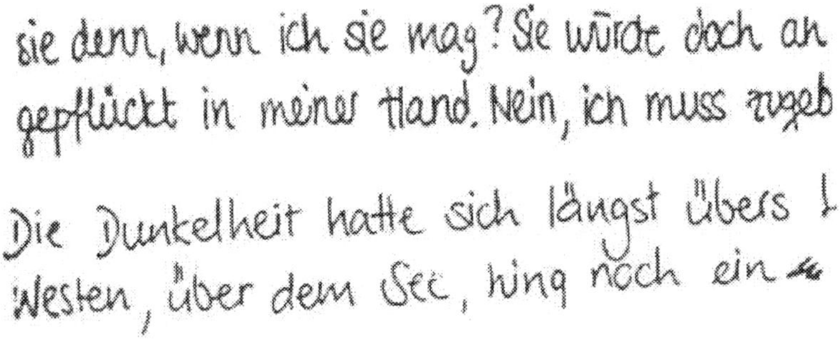

Fig. 87 Two women (identical twins) at age twenty

In another study R. T. Osborne noted in 1980 that the correlation between identical twins in terms of all personality traits (intelligence, interests, extraversion/introversion) are greater than the correlation between nonidentical twins.[29]

We can summarize the work by saying that although there is enormous similarity between twins—in particular between identical twins—in terms of their personality traits, the similarity is not as great as we might expect from their physical resemblance. "Certain role patterns may come about between twins, for example which one is more dominant or the face they present to the outside world, something that itself has an effect on their attitudes and personality traits."[30]

---

29 R. T. Osborne, *Black and White* (Athens, GA:, 1980).

30 K. Halder and U. Imoberdorf, "Ein- und zweieiige Zwillingen im Spiegel ihrer Handschrift," *Angewandte Graphologie und Persönlichkeitsdiagnostik* 55 (2007): 23.

6

---

*When studying a handwriting, it is a good
idea to line it up next to four or
five others in order to see how it behaves in society.*

—E. Magnat

Uses of Graphology

Personnel

The main application of graphological analysis is the recruitment of personnel for business. Both small and large companies, as well as personnel consultants and headhunters, use graphology , particularly when looking for executive staff.

The extent to which graphology is used to select staff varies in Europe. It is greatest in France, being taken into account in 85 percent of all decisions involving personnel, followed by Switzerland and the Benelux countries at around 70 percent, whereas it is only around 15 percent in Germany.

Normally a handwriting sample is requested only during the course of the recruitment process. In other words, an advertisement for a vacancy does not immediately ask for a sample to be submitted with the other documents making up an application.

A survey carried out among the members of the association of French consultant graphologists in 1991 clearly demonstrated that graphology is used mainly when looking for management staff. This was the response given by 104 of the 144 members. A total of 77 percent claimed to be rarely or never involved in the overall recruitment process, 73 percent provided information by telephone either frequently or occasionally, and 71 percent mostly supplied short analyses. Detailed reports were generally submitted by 72 percent of members (more than one response was possible).

In two-thirds of all cases, the clients of graphologists are personnel consultants or the companies themselves. On average, each member of the graphological association had thirty clients, who showed a high level of loyalty, with 55 percent claiming to receive regular work from the same firms.

In France, the following branches make use of graphology, listed in order of importance: industry, the banking and insurance sector, electronics, the service sector, and trade and commerce. The list of companies is long and includes names such as Helvetia-Versicherung, Hoffmann-La Roche, Fiat, KLM, Martinair, Novartis, Schweizerischer Bankenverein, and others.

A graphological analysis contains information about

- the overall personality (level, caliber, integrity, vitality, dynamics, and control)

- intellectual abilities (analysis/synthesis, overview, judgment, planning and organization, and creativity)

- potential for achievement (ability to cope with stress, stable motivation, stamina, and mobility)

- social skills (self-expression, contact with and ability to convince others, self-assertion, teamwork, leadership skills, and emotional responses)

- strengths and weaknesses

- perspectives for development

The graphological report generally makes a significant contribution to the decision-making process, as it eliminates uncertainties in the assessment of a candidate and may confirm or back up the client's own impressions. Information contained in the report pointing out the strengths and weaknesses of an applicant can already be taken into account when references are obtained.

For analysis, the graphologist requires a sample of original text, one page in length, including a signature as well as details about the writer's age, sex, and profession. In addition, comprehensive information should be provided about the requirements for the vacancy at the company so the graphologist can compare this with the candidate's qualifications based on the graphological report.

According to a judgment given by the Munich Labor Tribunal on April 14, 1975, a candidate indirectly consents to graphological analysis if he or she includes a sample of handwriting with the documents submitted in the application.

Graphology often comes in where classical personnel (psychometric) tests are no longer used. The graphologist Hans Knobloch points out:

"Persons who have to submit to testing are generally people at the start of their career, applicants in the middle of the corporate hierarchy. The higher up the ladder, the less often tests are used, and at a certain level they are entirely out of the question. The psychometric psychologist therefore does not generally come into contact with high-caliber personalities, characterized by enormous acquired power or unique achievements. Here the psychologist is thus simply lacking a certain worldly wisdom, something that is available to the graphologist. In the course of his work a 'truly successful graphologist' makes acquaintance with personalities of a much higher level than his own, persons with whom he would otherwise not have come into contact."[31]

---

31   H. Knobloch, *Was verrät uns die Handschrift*(Munich:Piper, 1991), 207 f.

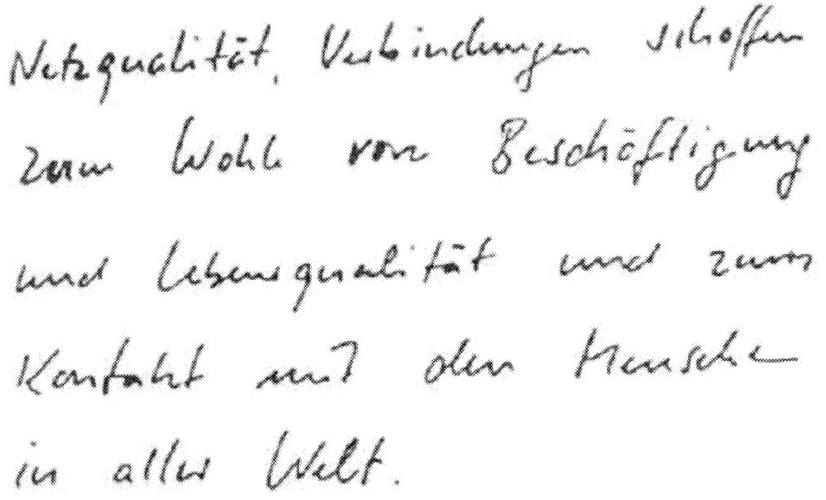

Fig. 88 The former CEO of Lufthansa, inventor of Star Alliance

Graphology of Children's and Adolescents' Handwriting

In 1878, Abbé Michon published *Fingerzeige über Kinderschriften*, which was translated into German in 1907. In this work he says, "Once the world has been convinced that the handwriting of a child is like a 'psychoscope,' allowing us to see into the most secret places of a child's soul, every mother, every caregiver who takes their responsibility seriously, will hasten to become a graphologist."

This comment by Michon is no less true today. Here the aim should be a graphological approach founded on anthropology that takes full account of the problems of development seen in young people.

The following authors have dealt with the question of children's handwriting: Ajuriaguerra, Avé-Lallemant, Gertrud Beschel, Minna Becker, Robert Bollschweiler, Jacqueline Peugeot, and Alois Legrün with more than 300(!) papers alone.

According to Minna Becker, the scribblings of preschool-age children unite "all possibilities of expressing character as in the bud of a flower." Anyone who has seen many such scribblings and has established a yardstick for the requirements involved by systematically comparing many attempts at writing will be amazed at what strength of expression is already shown by the basic dispositions of the infant character by such scribbling.

If a child's initial attempts at expression (scribbling) are above all assessed with the help of characteristic features, the instruction in writing offered at school undoubtedly opens up new possibilities for diagnosis that even today have not been sufficiently exploited by a long way.

It is an obvious truth in graphology that the analysis of children's handwritings calls for standards different from those for adults. Children's handwriting is basically also expressive, although the child's lack of writing skills makes analysis more difficult, albeit not impossible.

Experience has shown that teaching the copybook model at school will first cause children to focus on form in their handwriting. During their subsequent development, they will generally consider how to adapt the standardized model in line with their own picture of movement.

There have already been several attempts by graphologists to define specific developmental stages for handwriting as an aid to analyzing children's writings. Generally such categorizations into stages of handwriting are seen independently of the effective age of the child.

The most successful attempt to categorize children's handwriting into graphomotor age levels was made by Ajurriaguerra and his research group.[32] Proceeding from the assumption that a child's handwriting must be seen in comparison with children of the same age group or the same grade at school, it is not sufficient to solely relate it to adults' handwriting. After studies carried out at the Henri Rouselle children's hospital, thirty characteristics for children's handwritings were put

---

32 J. Peugeot, *La connaissance de l'enfant par l'écriture* (Paris: L'Harmattan, 2010), 91 ff.

together on a scale, with fourteen relating to form and sixteen to motor skills. A distinction is made between girls and boys, as girls are generally ahead of boys in terms of motor skills. Calculation of the graphomotor age is made using the extensive tables.

According to Legrün, reliable signs of maturity are as follows:

- form of connection—this progresses beyond the copybook model taught at school to gradually become more angular and then take on forms involving garlands or arcades

- signs of neglect/thready tailing-off of letter forms, clearly shown in the lowercase *s* and *z*.

The issues of left-handed writers and dyslexia are considered in detail in the relevant literature and cannot be dealt with further here.

Conflicts within the family or the social environment may produce corresponding signs in children's handwritings, described by Ursula Avé-Lallemant as distress signals.[33]

Their appearance always indicates that a child is in need of help. The research carried out by Avé-Lallemant with state funding resulted in the following fourteen signs of distress:

- Signs relating to writing space: disintegration of space, confusion of space, disorganization of space

- Signs relating to form: "meander" or square connection, end blockage, covering strokes, retouching

- Signs relating to movement: narrowness, slackening off of movement, stiffness of flow, muscle twitching (hyperkinesia)

- Signs relating to stroke: inelasticity of the forming stroke, pasty-dull stroke, breaks in stroke

---

33   U. Avé-Lallemant, *Notsignale in Schülerschriften* (Munich-Basel: E. Reinhardt, 1982).

We have to consider how pronounced such distress signals are in the handwriting sample. In other words, the level of distress in a child's handwriting needs to be correctly assessed. Another aspect is the length of time over which such signs are seen. Do signals of distress make only a temporary appearance (for example, during puberty) or can they be observed in the handwriting over an extended period?

Besides general aptitudes, the handwritings of adolescents also indicate specific abilities that are important for their subsequent choice of profession.

In handwriting we distinguish between the following:

- Talent for mathematics

- Talent for languages

- Theoretical talent

- Practical talent

- Technically productive talent

- Artistically productive talent

- Reproductive talent[34]

As the handwritings of children and adolescents are generally readily available, so-called longitudinal observation over a number of years is possible. However, we will rarely come across development that corresponds to the standard pattern, as shown by the many depictions provided by Avé-Lallemant.

Here too the graphologist dealing with the handwritings of children and adolescents will initially have to apply a relatively holistic approach—in other words, giving consideration to movement, form, and space.

---

34 The author of this book considers the handwriting of children and adolescents in detail in his course Aufbaukurs Graphologie. Cf. also R. Bollschweiler, *Berufsberatung und Graphologie* (Lucerne: 1989).

"In global terms it can be said that form expresses the skills and characteristic qualities of the personality, space the type and manner of social and cultural relationships, and movement the vital basis for writing," said Avé-Lallemant.[35]

At a graphological level, the change in the elasticity of the stroke is generally followed by an improvement in the quality of forms that is seen from age fifteen with cerebralization of the handwriting. By age eighteen the form level of a person's handwriting may already be fully developed.

In the above it is unfortunately possible to only touch on a number of subjects, which are discussed in detail in the literature cited, including numerous samples of handwriting.

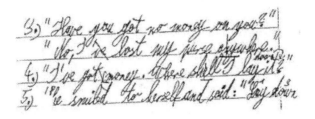

Fig. 89 The handwriting of a boy, age thirteen,
who was demoted at school.

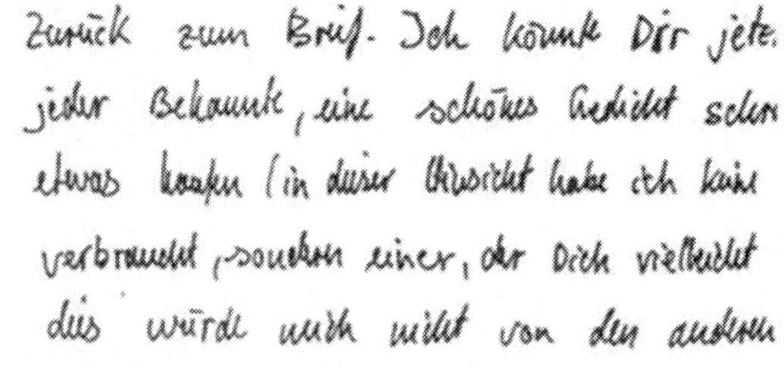

Fig. 90 The handwriting of a boy, age sixteen, doing well at school

35   U. Avé-Lallemant, *Graphologie des Jugendlichen*, vol. 2 (Munich/Basel: E. Reinhardt,1988), 76,

Reports on Compatibility (Partnerships)

Basically, *compatibility* may refer to either a business partnership or a private relationship. However, a graphologist is generally consulted in the second case, such as when a father wants an assessment of the relationship between his daughter and a former prisoner, when the mother of a young doctor wants to keep her son from marrying a nurse, or when a young man from Germany wants to marry a girl from the Philippines.

In all these cases it is essential to examine the handwritings of both partners to assess how they respond to each other. This is of course extremely difficult, as handwriting does not reveal the degree of sexual attraction as well as many environmental factors. For this reason, drawing up compatibility reports is a highly complex and time-consuming matter.

The identification of unconscious processes involved in the selection of a partner also calls for an extensive knowledge of depth psychology from the graphologist, in addition to an unbiased approach and a healthy relationship with oneself.

There are, however, a number of aspects that play a key role for the assessment of compatibility. In the author's experience the difference in social origin, education and so on of the two partners should not be too great or it may be doubtful from the outset how long the relationship will last. The form level of the handwritings will be helpful in this regard. The extent to which the partners will fall in love, and their "blindness" to each other, can easily be identified according to the graphological signs indicating strength of feeling or passion. The following factors also play a role: a willingness to adapt in relation to the ability to adapt, steadiness, and inconsistency. A writer who is steady by nature will be less attracted to conflict and thus more satisfied; however, he or she is also characterized by weaker drives and will therefore be less "interesting."

This results in a so-called "dominant handwriting" for the assessment of compatibility, namely that of the more difficult, also more inconsistent partner. For example, Picasso in Fig. 46 represents dominant handwriting; his partners always had to fit in with his needs. This approach is used to assess the ability to accept the inconsistent partner—that is, to determine the point at which excessive behavior can no longer be tolerated. Here all attributes are not judged per se, only how the other partner evaluates them.

The graphological analysis then assesses the extent to which the two temperaments are compatible, in terms of their emotional, mental, and sensual rapport.

Apart from the classic Freudian relationship patterns of compensation, projection, transference, identification, and so on, the four basic patterns of unconscious interaction between partners developed by Jürg Willi[36] are also useful for the purpose of graphological analysis: the narcissistic, oral, anal, and phallic-hysterical relationship patterns. For example, when selecting a partner, the narcissist wants to find a person who will idealize him or her and provide unconditional admiration in order to boost his or her ego and feelings of self-worth. The narcissist expects the partner, generally a submissive individual, to adapt so that the partner's life revolves entirely around the narcissist.

Although the graphologist cannot provide a guarantee for a lasting relationship, he or she can help clients avoid relationships laden with conflict and identify relationship patterns from his analysis of the overall situation: A person like Picasso (fig. 46) would never have been recommended as a husband.

Borderline Cases

The graphologist leaves safe ground when it is a question of discovering pathological features in handwriting: graphological analysis is not reliable in this regard. Previously it was assumed that mental illness

---

36 J. Willi, *Die Zweierbeziehung* (Reinbek nr. Hamburg: Rowohlt, 1996).

would be expressed in handwriting if it brought about a change in personality; however, that is not always the case.

According to the current knowledge of graphology, we can at most speak of a handwriting that is pathologically suspect. Most serious graphologists therefore refuse to diagnose a specific disease from handwriting.

"Whenever doctors are interested in graphology and take it up seriously or as a sideline, they wish to supplement their clinical picture of a patient and his disease by investigating his personality," graphologist Robert Heiss said. "There is an extensive collection of works, which have been written not only by graphologists but above all by doctors, dealing with the personality of patients showing the clinical symptoms of a disease. For example, we can find studies on the writing of patients suffering from tuberculosis and the handwriting of the heavy drinker.[37]

It has been repeatedly demonstrated that there no more exists a handwriting representative of tuberculosis patients than there exists one of the schizophrenic. Attempts have also been made to identify handwritings that are typical of heavy drinkers.

However, this result calls for qualification, as the handwriting typical of a heavy drinker can also be found in conjunction with other personality disorders—and there are even habitual drinkers whose handwriting looks perfectly normal. The same applies to identifying a tendency toward suicide in one's handwriting. As the graphological analysis of numerous suicide notes has demonstrated, it is possible to identify a tendency toward suicide, but it will not necessarily be apparent.[38]

---

37 R. Heiss, "Krankheit und Handschrift," *CIBA-Zeitschrift* 9, no. 98 (1960): 3269.

38 H. Ploog, "Zur Erkennung der Suiziddisposition aus der Handschrift," *Angewandte Graphologie und Charakterkunde*, no. 2 (1979): 42–53.

7

As long as handwriting is free and not constrained by copybook style, it
will almost always express the intrinsic character
of the writer in one manner or another.

—G. W. Leibniz

Validation of Graphology

The question here is whether the conclusions and assertions made after the analysis of a handwriting are objectively correct. This involves validation at the *level of interpretation,* something that has to date most frequently come in for criticism.

Over the last hundred years almost fifty doctoral theses on this subject have been submitted to faculties in many different disciplines in the German-speaking world. Hypotheses were formed on an empirical basis and correlated with tests or external criteria (= professional success).

Graphology considers personality as a functional—or in case of a personality disorder as a dysfunctional—unit. No other diagnostic tool in psychology offers a perspective comparable to graphology.

This excludes any direct and isolated graphological judgment on single "traits": judgments of this kind must be inferred from the whole personality structure. It follows that quantification procedures in graphology ought to be carried out on the level of entire personality evaluations. Therefore, it is an irresponsible approach to assign graphic traits to "lists of diagnostic indicators."

In a functional whole, the component parts have no significance apart from their position within that system of functioning. When a melody is transposed into another key, not a single note in it retains its identity; the melody, however, does.

According to graphologist Sonnemann:

> The reason for the academic resistance to graphology could
> be the "typical" scientist's comparative lack of specific
> aptitude for the adequate perception of pattern (gestalt)
> qualities which the typical student of art and aesthetics
> has no difficulty in recognizing in all their distinctness;
> rationalizing for this deficiency, the scientist is easily tempted
> to ascribe the "vagueness" of his experience of such qualities
> to the experienced object. (Sonnemann 1950)

"In some cases the result has already been influenced by the organizational
set-up of the investigation, especially when involving examiners with
a negative approach to graphology. (…) Inferior results can also be
observed when unqualified experts are consulted about studies."[39]

In 1945, Hans Jürgen Eysenck arrived at the following conclusion in the
British Journal of Psychology: "Taken together, these results seem to show
fairly conclusively that it is possible for a skilled graphologist to diagnose
personality traits from handwriting with better-than-chance success."

In global terms we can say that when the validity of graphology is
examined, it will offer results that are perfectly comparable with those
of other methods and will sometimes even surpass them.

In the field of psychology the interest in personality testing started to
decline around 1973 and was rekindled only in the form of theoretical
personality models by the "Big 5" at the beginning of the 1990s. Schuler
appears somewhat resigned to this in his summary of the situation:
"The available meta-analyses seem at present to generalize too strongly
about existing systematic influences. Perhaps we need to wait a few years
until sufficient primary studies have been carried out with direct Big 5
measurements."[40]

---

39 Robert Lewinsky, "Möglichkeiten und Grenzen der Graphologie in der klinisch-
diagnostichen Praxis" (Dissertation,., Zürich University, 1977) , 28.

40 Heinz Schuler, *Lehrbuch der Personalpsychologie,* (Göttingen: Hogrefe,, 2001), 115.

The term *meta-analysis* describes a technique for combining the empirical findings of different independent studies dealing with a single issue. A synthesis of graphological studies written in German was drawn up by Rainer Doubrawa in his dissertation titled "Handschrift und Persönlichkeit" for his PhD at the University of Bonn in 1978. This task was undertaken for the English-speaking world by Olivia Graham of London, in her article published in the journal *Angewandte Graphologie und Persönlichkeitsdiagnostik*, No. 2, 50th year, August 2002, p. 74–82. However, the language barrier means that all research reported in German is virtually unknown in England and the United States.

A number of important studies are listed below:

1. Wolf-Dieter Rasch: Hat sich die Graphologie bewährt? Hans Huber, Bern and Stuttgart 1957 (a study asking whether graphology has proved its worth)

The 114 graphological assessments carried out by the Institute of Psychology at the University of Freiburg were compared with the results obtained by assessors at a private firm in a questionnaire involving eighteen questions and scales of 1 to 6. These assessors had observed each employee at the company for some time. A control group was used to check the correlation between assessments. The assessments made by the different assessors at the firm for one of the employees showed an agreement of 79 percent, thereby demonstrating that the questionnaire was fit for its intended purpose.

Results		Question No.		Corr. coeff.
Highly significant	r > 0.28	5	Personal caliber	0.30
		7	Intellectual abilities	0.29
		17	Leadership potential	0.25

Significant	r > 0.24	4	Maturity	0.23
		18	Overall aptitude	0.23
		9	Practical skills	0.21
Non-significant	r > 0.18	16	Attitude toward colleagues	0.20
		11	Negotiating skills	0.17
Tendency	r > 0.15	8	Memory	0.12

The analysis of 114 cases resulted in around 75 percent agreement between the company assessors and the graphologists. The prognostic value of the graphological report before the appointment of new staff is first and foremost based on the overall aspects of the personality.

(This study, which was very painstaking in terms of method, is still available secondhand via the Internet.)

2. Langer, George: "Graphology in Personality Assessment: A Reliability and Validity Study," doctoral diss., Adelphi University, 1993.

The results obtained by two graphologists (Felix Klein and Roger Rubin) were compared with those of fourteen clinical psychologists (PhD students) under experimentally and methodologically rigorous conditions. The test subjects were twenty-one adults between eighteen and fifty-four who took part in a battery of standard clinical tests at Adelphi University's Derner Institute. Both the clinical psychologists and the graphologists were asked to complete the Q-data (Q = questionnaire) according to Block's California Q-Sort method (1978). This consists of 100 items describing personality on a scale from 1 to 9 (from the least to the most apt) and provides a quasi-normal distribution of descriptions.

The results of the study led to the conclusion that it is indeed possible to make accurate and reliable assessments of personality by means of handwriting analysis. The clinicians and graphologists were also generally in agreement where DSM-III-R diagnosis was concerned. All three hypotheses put forward by the study were confirmed, in particular the second hypothesis relating to the validity of the graphological Q-data. Significant positive correlations between 0.21 and 0.45 were established, without significant negative correlations being observed.

However, this method had the disadvantage that the questionnaire was strongly behavior oriented. It focused less on the subconscious and emotional or fantasy states. These are aspects that both clinical testing and handwriting analysis try to explore.

(The graphologist Felix Klein is unfortunately no longer alive, and it would be no easy matter to find someone else equally qualified to carry out a study along the same lines in the USA.)

3. S. Mouly, I. Mahé, K. Champion, C. Bertin, J. F. Bergmann. "Graphology for the Diagnosis of Suicide Attempts: A Blind Proof of Principle Controlled Study." In *International Journal of Clinical Practice*, March 2007, p. 411–415.

Forty patients admitted to two large hospitals in Paris after an attempt at suicide were asked to provide a sample of handwriting on their day of discharge. Each wrote a short letter describing a childhood memory while a control group of forty healthy volunteers were asked to do the same. Two graphologists and two physicians of internal medicine without any understanding of graphology or knowledge of either the patients or the control group then attempted to assign the samples, numbered in random order, to either the control or the patient group. The graphologists correctly identified thirty-two of the forty scripts as belonging to the patient group, whereas the score for the internal specialists was twenty-seven out of forty. In addition, the graphologists correctly identified thirty-three of forty scripts as belonging to the control group; the score for the internal specialists was thirty-four out of forty. The study then finished with the selection of twelve handwriting samples showing signs of sadness or sensitivity; 82 percent of these scripts were identified correctly by the graphologists and 71 percent by the internal specialists. Although the graphologists initially disagreed about twelve letters, they then reached the correct conclusion in eight cases after consultation. This study thus offers a gratifying level of accuracy, suggesting that graphology could successfully be used as an additional instrument for decision making in the field of psychiatry or internal medicine.

(In the study the graphologists did not concern themselves with individual characteristics but with global features or syndromes of features.)

---

4. Calvin J. Frederick: An Investigation of Handwriting of Suicide Persons through suicide notes, Journal of Abnormal Psychology, 1968, Vol. 73, No. 3, 263 - 267

The question of whether or not the handwriting of persons who commit suicide and leave a note could be distinguished from controls was examined by employing 3 sets of judges: professional graphologists of Europe, American detectives, and secretaries. A total of 180 notes comprised 45 sets, each consisting of one original note plus three control handwritten copies placed in loose-leaf binders on separate pages. Position of the original note of each set in the binders was arranged according to the table of random numbers. The actual suicide notes were not seen by the control writers who wrote from a typewritten copy replicated on a plain 5 x 8 in. card so as to prevent the control Ss from seeing the handwriting of the original note, thereby preventing any contamination effects. Although the typed cards contained replications of the original notes line for line, including placement of the words to the line, misspelled words, incorrect capitalizations, words crossed out, etc., the control writers were permitted to write the notes in their own natural style as far as the writing went.

The graphology judges were all fully qualified European graphologists trained at the universities of Berlin, Freiburg, Stockholm, Basel and Munich. One was a former university professor.

Results: As may be seen from table 1 (not shown here) the five experimental judges (graphologists) all exceeded chance in selecting genuine suicide notes by a strikingly significant margin, far beyond the usual .001 level. Since the baseline provided was one genuine note out of every four, the 10 control judges did not exceed chance expectation, although 3 judges came close to it. While the judges did not agree among themselves in total ranking for all notes, there were significant findings where all judges were correct and in complete agreement in their accurate choices of the genuine notes. Graphologists all agreed correctly in 14 out of 45 selections or 31 %; detectives were all correct in 3 out of 45, or 6 %; and secretaries were all correct in 2 out of 45, or 4 %.

---

5. Claudia Caspers: Ring Trials in Handwriting Analysis, www.schriftanalyse-validierung.info

---

Ring trials in graphology started in Germany 2015 and are intended to assure scientific quality and the evaluation of graphology and handwriting expertise by establishing accuracy during comparative and repeated testing. In a ring trial participants will get identical handwritings and test (1) independently of one another, (2) within a limited time period, (3) with their respective methods (e.g. manual, with software, physical/technical examination), (4) according to provided and/or defined criteria (choice or specific handwriting features and/or specific personality traits).

In ring trial 003 from 2017 data were collected by means of questionnaire technique and graphologically from the handwritings of 53 persons. Questionnaires in method 1 established a self-image with four personality trait parameters (internal security, initiative, conflict optimism, flexibility) of 53 tested persons. Method 2 captured an external image with five personality trait parameters (empathy, conflict skills, creativity, balance, integrity) with an average of three external assessors per self-assessor (a total of 152 colleagues and friends or relatives), also by means of questionnaires. Thus a total of nine personality trait parameters were obtained for each participating person, which were being assessed by a pool of eight graphologists (the author of this book included) and a software-based method (GraphoPro).

The results in detail can be looked up under the above mentioned web address in English language. Especially striking is the fact that the graphologists achieved a higher agreement with the self-assessment than with external assessments by colleagues and friends. Which is not surprising as graphologists get closer to the core of a personality than any external assessment. Also surprising was that the software-based method achieved as positive results as the classic manual graphological method. The agreement was high for both measuring methods used (Kendall and percentage rank comparison agreement). These ring trials are being continued.

A Few Sample Analyses

Sample 1

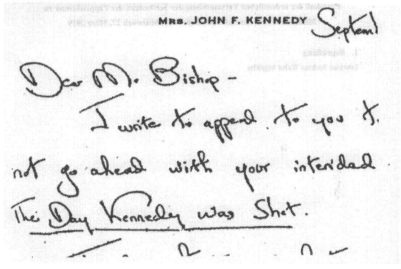

MRS. JOHN F. KENNEDY

Dear Mr. Bishop –
I write to appeal to you to
not go ahead with your intended
The Day Kennedy was Shot.

Fig. 91 Jacqueline Kennedy, at age 38

Jacqueline Kennedy

The script at the age of 38 shows a personality made up with composure and self-control, pride and ambition, together with a certain feminine vanity. She acts in a very conscious and careful way, following aesthetical and ethical guiding images. She has an individual sense for style and beauty, however more imitating others than creative in her own way. A drive for individual fulfillment, independence and aplomb, ambitiously traced, can also be seen. She is well versed and extraverted in the company of others; in face-to-face contact however she is rather formal and inhibited. She sees herself more spirited and more open than she really is. In fact she is considerably insecure and has a strong need for safety, which is the reason for her formal attitude in the search to stabilize herself. Sensuality and joie de vivre can hardly be seen in the handwriting. The field of emotions and closeness to nature is excluded and she fills this gap with intellectual and aesthetical pursuits.

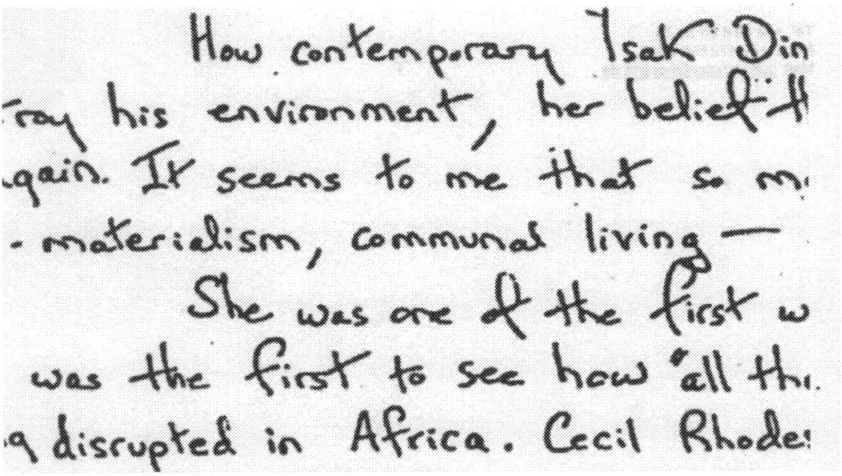
How contemporary Isak Din
ray his environment, her belief th
gain. It seems to me that so m
- materialism, communal living —
She was one of the first w
was the first to see how all th
g disrupted in Africa. Cecil Rhodes

Fig. 91a Jacqueline Kennedy, at age 60

The second script at age 60 shows the development of her personality, but also the limitations of her inner growth. She is better integrated in her environment and keeps less distance to others, although reserve, tactfulness and consciousness are still predominant. Her personal needs are still subdued in favour of strong intellectual and spiritual interests. Pride plays a lesser role. The writer seems mentally more stable and better balanced. These changes are connected with the stabilization of her ego and her improved self-assuredness. The sensual, emotional and libidinal parts of her personality have still not been developed in a noticeable way. The development potentialities were limited and onesided, which could already be surmised from her earlier writing.

Graphological comments: The handwriting shows left slant and a strong emphasis on the initial letters (more samples of her handwriting can be found on google images). The letters in the middle zone look like print script and are not connected. The change in her later handwriting is obvious: her handwriting is much smaller including the initial letters. The handwriting is still unconnected and left slant is still prevailing.

Sample 2:

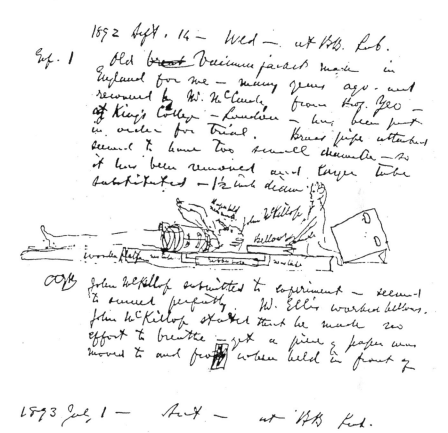

Fig. 92 Alexander Graham Bell, fifty-one, second president of the National Geographic Society

The writer is primarily influenced by his thinking function. At an intellectual level he can absorb rapidly and with above-average agility. He forms independent judgments from positive experience. His direction of interest tends outward—that is, his clear and, at the same time, abstract way of thinking in combination with a strong intellectual and emotional commitment lead him to master concrete problems. His easily stimulated thought process allows him to expediently simplify and reduce various factors to their core or essence. He is an observer, generally unbiased but nonetheless critical, with a good capacity for intellectual processing. His thinking moves into analytical depths as well as in a synthesizing direction, and a wide horizon of consciousness provides him with multiple directions of thought. Strong intuitive coloring shows that his subconscious influences his thinking, which makes it possible to find creative solutions.

He is a good negotiator, approaching people openly and spontaneously. In short, he handles people well with a relaxed and natural manner. His performance behavior is determined by goal-oriented work based on a capacity for effort, toughness, and assertion. From case to case, he could have an extensive performance with improvisation as well as an intensive, precise procedure. His activity is powered by specific ambition, the joy of enterprise, and the strong desire to expand his area of influence. He is at times impatient, very spontaneous, and fully committed.

Graphological comments: This script is small and simplified with rapid connections. It slants to the right with a strong emphasis on movement, with the middle zone being rather small at the expense of the upper and lower lengths. The main form of connection is the garland. By immediately connecting the lower lengths rightward to the next letter, the writer indicates that he is highly efficient in his work. The rhythm of his progression across the page is somewhat uneasy despite the otherwise satisfactory form level.

Sample 3

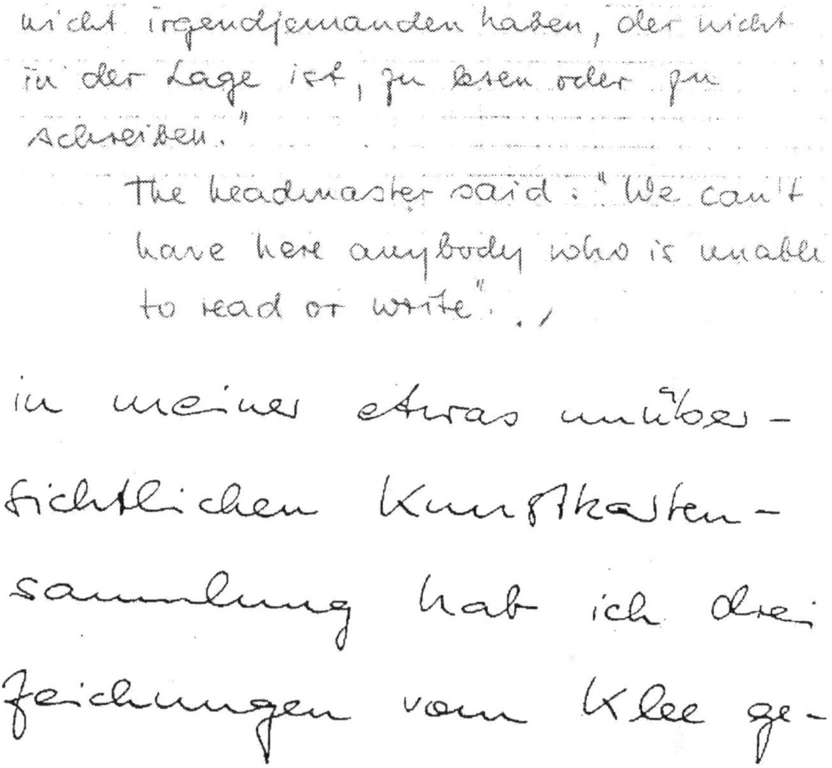

nicht irgendjemanden haben, der nicht in der Lage ist, zu lesen oder zu schreiben."

The headmaster said: "We can't have here anybody who is unable to read or write".

in meiner etwas unüber-sichtlichen Kunstkasten-sammlung hab ich drei Zeichnungen vom Klee ge-

Fig. 93 The first handwriting was provided by a twenty-nine-year-old woman who was employed as a secretary at the time. The second script was written eighteen years later. She now works as a yoga teacher and art dealer. During this period of time she experienced several partnerships and took part in numerous workshops as well as psychotherapy lasting three years.

The first handwriting sample shows a woman who is very open, aware of her responsibilities, and makes an effort to fit in. Reliable, friendly, and very amiable, this writer has no problem in making contact and getting along with others.

As shown in the second handwriting, she has managed in the meantime to reduce her willingness to conform. She has no doubt been helped by not only recognizing her personal motives and conditioning, but above all by a more instinctive orientation toward her inner world. She has let her unconscious strengths come into play and accepts her intuition as a valuable asset. Her approach is now less restricted and more tolerant.

Compared with before, there has also been an increase in the writer's vitality and general level of excitability. A certain inhibition and suppression of unconscious instincts and desires have faded away, allowing her to live life more fully. Sensible virtues and feminine conformity have given way to the ability to take charge of her life and fulfill herself as a woman. A comparison of the two samples confirms that this writer has undergone a very positive development in recent years. She used to be "low maintenance" and conventional—today she is not so easy to handle, but she is more interesting to know. Now that she has achieved self-realization, she has clearly become a more rounded person.

Graphological comments: The first handwriting looks very inhibited. It is more regular and not as rapid as the second sample. The stroke is also not nearly as strong. Overall, the form level of the handwriting has matured, giving the writer a better quality of life. In the second sample the stroke is more forceful and intense, showing relaxed garlands and an emphasis on movement. Overall, the writing looks less regular and not as tense.

***

Instructions for completing the graphological worksheet (see overleaf).

1. Enlarge the form to DIN A4.

2. Give at least five characteristic features each for the picture of space, form, and movement.

3. Assess the five global features.

4. Your ratings for the individual variables should be marked with a circle in the relevant column. The middle column stands for a handwriting executed according to the school model (size, proportions, and so on). For example, column 1 stands for "quite fast," column 2 for "fast," and column 3 for "very fast." When you have finished, join up the circles with a line.

The left columns of the worksheet correspond to contraction and the right columns to release. If a person exhibits a considerable contraction tendency, he or she is hemmed in by rational control. "On the other hand, if his writing is very released, he is lacking in mental control to such an extent that his emotions carry him away" (Lewinson 1942). For a comparison see also Klara B. Roman's worksheet, it serves the same purpose (Roman 1952).

Graphological Worksheet

Writer:　　　　Age:　Occupation:　　　　Date:　For:

First impression:

A) Global examination

    I.   Relation between movement and form:

    II. Pophal's degree of tension:

    III. Rhythm (movement, form, space):

    IV. Degree of individuality:

    V. Homogeneity (movement, form, space):

B) Individual graphic variables:

		3	2	1	0	1	2	3		Special remarks
I	Slowness								Speed	
	Disconnected writing								Connected writing	
	Small writing								Large writing	
	Simplification								Enrichment	
	Meager forms								Full forms	
	Sharpness								Pastiness	
II	Stroke in relief								Unvarying stroke	
	Pressure								Lack of pressure	
	Regularity								Irregularity	
	Angle								Thread, double curve	
	Narrowness								Wideness	
III	Arcade								Garland	
	Left trend								Right trend	
	Left slant								Right slant	
IV	Lower lengths > upper lengths								Upper lengths > lower lengths	
	High middle zone								Low middle zone	
	Word beginnings emphasized								Word beginnings minimized	
	Word endings emphasized								Word endings minimized	
V	Organized								Unorganized	
	Word distance > line distance								Line distance > word distance	

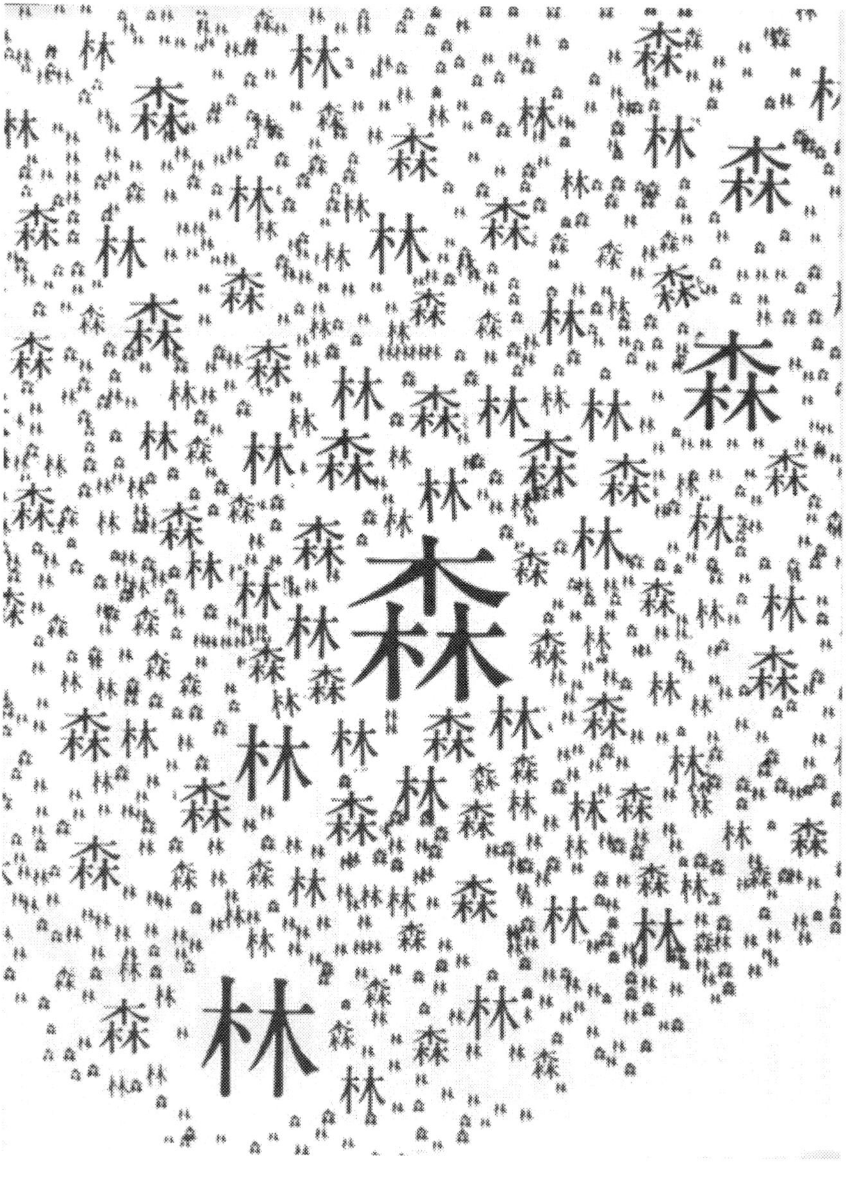

Test Questions

Please select the correct answer (several answers are possible):

1. **A professional handwriting analysis allows conclusions to be drawn relating to**

    a) general predispositions of the writer in terms of thinking, emotions, and will.

    b) specific diseases.

    c) age and gender.

    d) degree of maturity of his personality.

2. **The copybook model learned at school by the writer is for the graphologist**

    a) of no interest as it is the same for everyone.

    b) important, because it allows the independence of the writer to be assessed depending on whether he or she keeps to this model.

    c) important in the case of foreign handwritings because different conventions apply in each country.

    d) of secondary relevance because of trends in handwriting.

3. **The signature**

   a) offers no scope for making statements about vanity and self-presentation.

   b) shows the personality as the writer would like to be.

   c) does not generally differ from the text.

   d) provides no pointers for graphological analysis, as it is legally binding.

4. **An illegible handwriting can indicate**

   a) rejection of social norms.

   b) transparency on the part of the writer.

   c) a lack of consideration for others.

   d) little effort to comply with set standards and clarity.

5. **The handwriting in Fig. 39 is**

   a) characterized by form.

   b) dominated by movement.

   c) contains disintegrated forms.

   d) contains threadlike connections.

6. **The layout of a handwriting includes the following elements:**

   a) line spacing

   b) word spacing

   c) lined paper

   d) clearly delineated letters

7. **The good form level of the handwriting shown in Fig. 86 is caused by**

   a) good connections between letters.

   b) good rhythm.

   c) numerous simplifications.

   d) the individuality of the letterforms.

8. **Displaced pressure is said to exist when**

   a) there is pressure on the horizontal at the end of a word.

   b) pressure can be seen on the downstroke.

   c) the handwriting looks muddy.

   d) pressure can be seen on the upstroke.

9. **The following forms of connection can be seen in the handwriting shown in Fig. 76:**

   a) arcades

   b) threads and angles

   c) garlands

   d) double curves.

10. **The handwriting shown in Fig. 65**

   a) has a strong emphasis on form.

   b) has a good layout.

   c) is written in haste.

   d) has a strong emphasis on movement.

Answers

1 a, d; 2 b, c; 3 b; 4 a, d; 5 b, c, d; 6 a, b; 7 b, d; 8 a, d; 9 b, c; 10 c, d

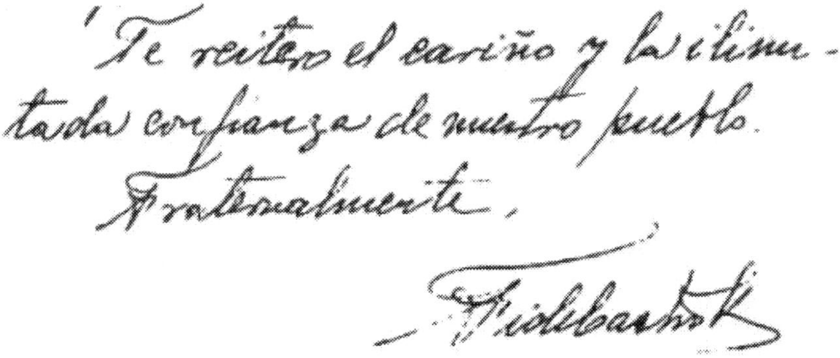

Fig. 94 Angles and right slant can be seen in
the handwriting of Fidel Castro.

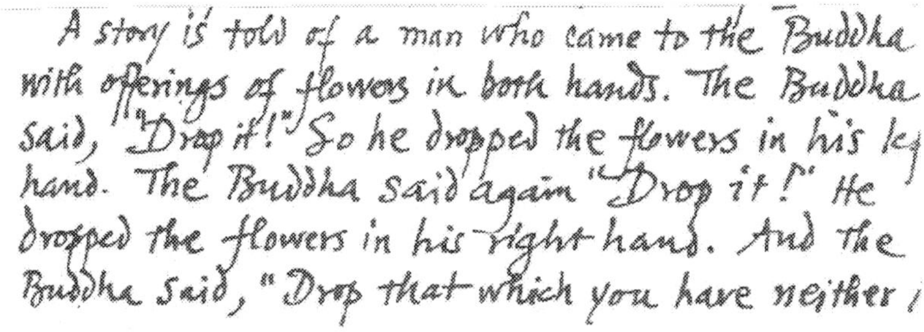

Fig. 95 High form level in the handwriting of Alan Watts

Graphological Aphorisms

Writing above all means carrying out a task. But writing is a whole lot more. Handwriting allows us to move from material dependence to the intangible universe of the mind: the world of imagination, will, ideas, wishes and guiding images. A universe that is subject to laws other than in the material world. Writing is thus an activity that is very human and extraordinarily illuminating, a sort of model for the human condition in itself. The dual polarity of man manifests itself through involvement in movement and form in handwriting.

W. H. MÜLLER and A. ENSKAT

The American President Lincoln said to his staff, "A man of 40 is responsible for his face." This means that a "man of 40" is also responsible for his handwriting: in each aspect that goes to make up the (form) level of the writing.

U. AVÉ-LALLEMANT

The more I compare the different handwritings I come across, the more I believe that an equal number of expressions and manifestations of the writer's character have to be described.

J. W. v. GOETHE

Every good graphological portrait is in fact summed up in the first and the last sentence. The rest is made up of details and nuances.

E. MAGNAT

There are handwritings that know where they are going, and there are others that dawdle along. Not all travelers take the same path but they are all following one road. People out for a walk on the other hand wander about to a greater or lesser extent. Some to gaze at the countryside, others set off on a voyage of self-discovery while a few just want to forget themselves.

E. MAGNAT

When a graphologist follows the trace of a handwriting, he will soon render an account of where the writer is heading for, whether he has a goal, whether he is dawdling along, is looking for himself or is trying to escape.

E. MAGNAT

Bibliography

Beauchataud, Gabrielle. *Learn Graphology.* London, 1988 (Reprint).

Bernard, Marie. *The Art of Graphology.* New York, 1985.

Blanqufort D'anglards, Madeleine. *Motivations & Compensations, Graphological & Psychological Approaches.* Tucson, AZ, 2004.

Caille, Emile. *Characters and Handwriting.* London, 1991 (Reprint).

Carmi, A., and Schneider, S. (Ed.). *Experiencing Graphology.* London, 1968.

Gille-Maisani, Jean-Charles. *The Psychology of Handwriting.* London 1992.

Huntington, Hartford. *You Are What You Write.* New York, 1973.

Jacoby, Hans. *Analysis of Handwriting.* London, 1991 (Reprint).

Klein, Felix. Gestalt Graphology, New York (Iuniverse) 2007.

Nezos, Renna. *Graphology.* London ,1986.

———. *Advanced Graphology.* London, 1993.

Pettinatti, Graziella. Je Lie Les Lettres, Montreal (Trécarré) 2008.

Peugeot, J., Lombard, M., De Noblens. *Manual of Graphology.* London, 1997.

Pulver, Max. *The Symbolism of Handwriting.* London, 1994 (Reprint).

Roman, Klara. *Handwriting: A Key to Personality.* New York, 1952.

Saudek, Robert. *The Psychology of Handwriting.* London, 1954.

Schweighofer, Fritz: *Graphology and Psychoanalysis.* New York ,1979.

Seifer, Marc. *The Definitive Book of Handwriting Analysis.* Franklin Lakes, 2009.

Semler-Delmar, Betty. *Schematic Graphology.* Winnetka, IL, 1987.

Sonnemann, Ulrich. *Handwriting Analysis.* New York, 1950.

Steer, Beverly, K. "Handwriting Measurement: A Psychometric Path to Personality." In *Graphological Papers.* Tohoku Fukushi University, Sendai, 1993.

Stein Lewinson, Thea, and Zubin, Joseph. *Handwriting Analysis.* New York, 1942.

Stein Lewinson, Thea. "Classic Schools of Graphology." In Baruch Nevo (Ed.), *Scientific Aspects of Graphology.* Springfield, IL, 1986,

Teillard, Anna. *The Soul and Handwriting.* London, 1993 (Reprint),

Teltscher, H. O. *Handwriting—Revelation of the Self.* New York, 1971,

Tulloch, Alex. *Szondi's Theory of Personality in Handwriting.* London, 1990,

Victor, Frank. Handwriting: A Personality Projection. Eugene, OR, 1989 (Reprint).

Wolff, Werner. *Diagrams of the Unconscious.* New York, 1948.

Yalon, Dafna, and Danor, Rudi. *Towards Scientific Graphology.* London, 1992.

Yalon, Dafna (Ed.). *Graphology Across Cultures,* Hampton Hill, 2003.

Many reprints and secondhand and out-of-print books are available from the British Academy of Graphology and the British Institute of Graphologists.

Professional associations on the Internet:

UNITED STATES: American Society of Professional Graphologists (ASPG/New York): www.aspghandwriting.org

CANADA: Association des Graphologues du Québec
www.graphoquebec.com

UNITED KINGDOM: The British Academy of Graphology (BAOG/London):
www.graphology.co.uk

FRANCE: Société Française de Graphologie (SFDG/Paris):
www.graphologie.asso.fr

GERMANY: Professional Association of Certified Graphologists/Psychologists
(PACG/Munich): www.graphologie.de

ISRAEL: The Society for Scientific Graphology
www.graphology.dpages.co.il

ITALY: Agif Associazione Italo-Francese di Grafologia
www.agif-grafologia.it

Index

Printed in the United States
By Bookmasters